CONTENDING WITH
KENNAN

CONTENDING WITH
KENNAN

Toward a Philosophy
of American Power

Barton Gellman

PRAEGER SPECIAL STUDIES • PRAEGER SCIENTIFIC

New York • Philadelphia • Eastbourne, UK
Toronto • Hong Kong • Tokyo • Sydney

Library of Congress Cataloging in Publication Data

Gellman, Barton D., 1960–
  Contending with Kennan.

  Bibliography: p.

  1. Kennan, George Frost, 1904–   . 2. United
States — Foreign relations — Philosophy.   3. Politics and
war.   I. Title.
E748.K374G35   1984   327.73'001   84-4553
ISBN 9-03-063819-4 (alk. paper)
ISBN 0-03-006192-X (pbk)

Published in 1984 (hb) and 1985 (pb) by Praeger Publishe
CBS Educational and Professional Publishing, a Division of CBS In
521 Fifth Avenue, New York, NY 10175 U.
© 1984 by Barton Gellm

56789   052   9876543

Printed in the United States of America on acid-free pap

INTERNATIONAL OFFICES

Orders from outside the United States should be sent to the appropriate address listed below. Orders from areas
listed below should be placed through CBS International Publishing, 383 Madison Ave., New York, NY 10175 U

Australia, New Zealand
Holt Saunders, Pty, Ltd., 9 Waltham St., Artarmon, N.S.W. 2064, Sydney, Australia

Canada
Holt, Rinehart & Winston of Canada, 55 Horner Ave., Toronto, Ontario, Canada M8Z 4X6

Europe, the Middle East, & Africa
Holt Saunders, Ltd., 1 St. Anne's Road, Eastbourne, East Sussex, England BN21 3UN

Japan
Holt Saunders, Ltd., Ichibancho Central Building, 22-1 Ichibancho, 3rd Floor, Chiyodaku, Tokyo, Japan

Hong Kong, Southeast Asia
Holt Saunders Asia, Ltd., 10 Fl, Intercontinental Plaza, 94 Granville Road, Tsim Sha Tsui East, Kowloon,
Hong Kong

**Manuscript submissions should be sent to the Editorial Director, Praeger Publishers, 521 Fifth Avenue,
New York, NY 10175 USA**

*To my parents
and my stepfather*

Contents

Foreword

On February 16, 1984, George Frost Kennan began his 81st year. He has had two full careers: the first as one of the most effective and influential diplomats ever to serve the United States, the second as an historian of diplomacy and as a searching analyst of the dilemmas of contemporary foreign policy. At a time of life when most men and women have ceased to labor, he continues—and with increasing passion—to write and speak on the largest issues of our era, particularly the relationship between the United States and the Soviet Union and the threat to mankind posed by the arsenals of mass destruction that each possesses. Moreover, it is not merely Kennan's trenchant analysis of our contemporary predicaments that has earned him an ever-larger following. He is, as well, a true master of English prose. There is no one in American public life, and very few persons in American letters, whose mode of expression is more lucid.

Throughout his long working lifetime Kennan has been preoccupied with the phenomenon of Soviet power in the vast domains of the former Russian Empire. The Bolshevik seizure of power took place during his early adolescence. When he entered the Foreign Service in 1926, Lenin had been dead only two years. Twenty years later, nearing the apex of his diplomatic career, Kennan wrote the papers which, initially as confidential reports and later as public statements—including, most notably, the pseudonomous 1947 "X-Article" in *Foreign Affairs*—provided the doctrinal framework for the posture of containment that has guided

American policy toward the USSR ever since. Subsequently, as the first (and surely the most creative and distinguished) Director of the Policy Planning Staff of the Department of State, as United States Ambassador in Moscow, and then—his second career—as Professor in the School of Historical Studies at the Institute for Advanced Study, Kennan has tried again and again to elucidate for his own countrymen "the sources of Soviet conduct" (the title he gave to the "X" article).

Yet, as Barton Gellman argues in the pages that follow, while it is Russia and Soviet power that have provided a subject for so much of Kennan's writing, it is the use (and misuse) of American power that has been the source of his deepest underlying concern. Gellman notes that Kennan has never doubted that wise diplomacy on the part of the United States could shape a relationship with Moscow that would allow both nations to pursue their legitimate interests without war between them. But Kennan has long worried that American leaders and the public that elects them are not capable of sustaining a foreign policy that is steady and firm and yet flexible and moderate—and of doing so, moreover, not for a season or even for a presidential term, but year in and year out. An oft-repeated theme in Kennan's work is that because American statecraft is so often inconsistent and lacking in balance, the United States is both less effective and more bellicose than it need be. American bellicosity, in turn, merely serves to inspire similarly truculent Soviet behavior. As a consequence, so Kennan has argued repeatedly in recent years, the risk of war between the two superpowers—a war that inevitably would be fought with nuclear weapons—has become unacceptably great.

Kennan regards his role since leaving the Foreign Service in 1953 as primarily that of an historian. But he is very much a theorist of American power (although he himself would reject the label), and Gellman's book treats him explicitly as such. Gellman carefully displays the many strands of Kennan's thought about the nature and purposes of American power and shows how they fit together. Sometimes, Gellman points out, they do not fit. But he makes clear that Kennan's contradictions are themselves always worth exploring, for they elucidate the multiplicity of goals with which the managers of American foreign policy are nearly always confronted and the relative paucity of instruments available for achieving them.

Where Gellman disagrees with Kennan he does not hesitate to say so. That is another reason his book is worth reading. For it is not only a judicious analysis of Kennan's voluminous writings (published and unpublished) regarding American power, but it can be read also as an effort by a much younger person to come to terms with the many facets of that power. Gellman himself was born on November 3, 1960. He reached political awareness only during the administrations of Gerald Ford and Jimmy Carter; his Princeton undergraduate education extended well into the administration of Ronald Reagan. For him and his contemporaries, the Vietnam war—the most wrenching test of American power since World War II—is largely the stuff of history books, as is the Nixon/Kissinger effort to forge a detente with Moscow. Politics as usual for Americans of Gellman's age means a U.S.–Soviet relationship charged with tension and a perception that for the leaderships of both societies nuclear war is all too thinkable.

Gellman's book should not be read as his (let alone his generation's) "answer" to Kennan, unless the mere fact that he has found Kennan's thought so worthy of careful study is construed as an answer of sorts. Gellman is much too aware of the degree to which Kennan's conclusions are rooted in a profound knowledge of history that he himself cannot possibly yet have acquired. (That awareness may, incidentally, itself be a characteristic of Gellman's generation; someone of his age writing a decade earlier might have chosen a different stance and a different voice.)

Gellman is not only a careful analyst and respectful critic. Like Kennan himself, he is also a remarkably felicitous writer. He is already an accomplished journalist who has held reporting jobs on *The Miami Herald* and *The Washington Post* and whose articles have appeared in *The New Republic* and *National Journal*. His own style thus does justice to Kennan's. His book is a pleasure to read. One comes away from it with deeper understanding of the diplomat and scholar whose work it so thoughtfully examines, and with admiration for the author who has brought it forward.

Richard H. Ullman

Princeton, New Jersey
October 19, 1983

Preface

To nearly anyone with an opinion on the subject, it seems plain that there have been two George F. Kennans. There was Kennan the cold warrior, the Mr. "X" of 1947, who sounded alarms about the Soviets and plotted the strategy of "containment." Now, popularly, there is Kennan the peacemonger, the dovish historian and virtual isolationist who confines his public statements to exhortations against nuclear arms. The contrast puzzles casual critics. Some see Kennan today as a chastened convert to peaceful coexistence, a man who justly repudiates a hawkish past. Others, with other ideologies, see Kennan as a soldier who has lost his nerve and the courage of his convictions. What the critics agree on, and what is so widely believed that it amounts to the standard wisdom, is that some time between the Second World War and today George Kennan shed one political skin and grew another. Kennan's past and present beliefs, it is said, are inconsistent and irreconcilable.

It is a central argument of this book that the standard wisdom—along with most of the psychobiographical speculation that flows from it—is simply wrong. The two George Kennans, on closer inspection, are little more than caricatures, dimensionless cardboard cut-outs fashioned by partisans to flash at one another in policy debate. These portray nothing of the subtlety and the systematic nature of Kennan's political thought. My aim has been to begin such a systematic discussion, along with a critical appraisal, of Kennan's views on American power.

My point of departure is that Kennan has intended to be consistent in what he wrote and said, and that his claim to consistency should be taken seriously by readers who wish to understand him. Kennan's views do not all fit neatly together—quite—but a careful look will often show that what first appears to be contradictory is not so, in light of some hidden or imperfectly stated assumption of the argument. Where I found myself unable to resolve logical difficulties in this way, I looked for some explanation of how Kennan could have neglected them. The result, I think, is a good deal more revealing than the sort of criticism that points accusingly at ideas in tension and then regards the inquiry as closed.

I should say at the outset that Kennan, though he little knows it, has colluded in his misportrayal. A diplomat and a historian by training, Kennan is not so much un- as antitheoretical. He is darkly suspicious of ideologies and doctrines, and he goes to great lengths to avoid writing abstractly. He speaks more often of events than of trends, of exceptions than of rules, of prudence than of principles. He aligns himself more with "splitters" than with "lumpers" among historians. He makes it excessively difficult, on the whole, to see his views in broad relief. So doing, he has allowed his views to be seized upon by every sort of doctrinaire.

All this means that, as one critic justly charged, the business of isolating Kennan's premises amounts to something like archeology. His views (on, among other things, morality, democracy, and armed force) must be inferred and collected as fragments scattered in layers through his writing over time. The collector of these fragments will want to fit them together, like the paleontologists's museum display. Their configuration, though, is a puzzle. Even once you have built a plausible skeleton for Kennan's foreign policy and begun to flesh it out, you can never be sure that there is not a joint out of place or a rib stuck in where the tailbone ought to be. At the end of the exercise, worst of all, you may find you are left with a few extra pieces, which seem to fit nowhere. Where this has happened, or where the parts have added up to a rather awkward-looking animal, I have said so.

The motivating assumptions behind all my sifting and puzzling are two: that Kennan would appear on any short list of influential thinkers on American foreign policy, and that he is nonetheless very poorly understood. Kennan would much rather be remembered as a historian than a *philosophe*, and he dislikes to answer his critics, in part because of a surprising aversion to controversy. But it seems time to start setting the record straight. If this whole exercise is, in some ways, undertaken against Kennan's will, it is nonetheless fair to ask of a man who is given to displaying bits and pieces of his vision of foreign affairs that he account for the composite picture that develops over the years.

For truest colors in rendering Kennan I have usually thought it best to stick closely to his own words. It can be risky business to summarize him, and my method has generally been to look for the whole by arranging the parts before the eye. Kennan is nothing if not a superb stylist, and so direct quotation has the added virtue of a good read.

What has impressed me most in assessing Kennan is not his style but the continuing power of the themes he first struck three, four, and five decades ago. Kennan and I, after all, are virtually from different epochs. When Kennan was 22 and a year or so out of Princeton, as I am now, he looked out upon a world of a few dozen nations and felt the aftershocks of World War I in the rhythm of his own daily life. He could not yet guess there might be a second war like it; he had barely heard, if at all, of Korea; Vietnam was not even a name on the map. The Great Depression and New Deal were still in prospect. Lenin, Weber, Proust were the obituaries of the day. Women's suffrage was in its infancy, where it existed at all. Mussolini was just consolidating his power; Hitler had years of obscurity still before him. The frontier of technology was the transatlantic phone call and the transatlantic flight. There was no television, no plastic, no computer, no penicillin, no atom bomb. So much that defines my world was not dimly imagined in his; so much that defined his world has since been recorded and replaced. The wonder is not, in the end, that some of Kennan's judgments have been undermined by the headlong pace of change, but rather that the body of his work retains to this day so much of its persuasive force.

Barton Gellman

Oxford, England
September 1983

Acknowledgments

I am doubly indebted to Professor Richard H. Ullman of Princeton University, my teacher and friend: first for supervising my undergraduate thesis, then for encouraging me to publish it. Without his sharp criticism at the early stages, this would be a far sloppier book; without his later efforts on my behalf, it would probably not a be a book at all.

There are other debts on this book, more than I can mention. Patrick Bernuth and the editors at Praeger gave their confidence to a first-time author and guided me patiently through publication. George F. Kennan, both in correspondence and in person, kindly allowed me to interrupt his work on several occasions. Miles Kahler, Cyril Black, and Robert C. Tucker helped with early advice on organization. The Woodrow Wilson School of Public and International Affairs provided a grant to support my research and helped make possible the thesis; the Rhodes Trust has given me the luxury of time to think further and to revise it. Librarians at *The Washington Post*, *The New York Times* Washington bureau, and the Seeley G. Mudd Library (which houses the Kennan Papers) have all been generous with their time and resources.

A dozen friends helped me through the project at various stages, directly and indirectly. Michele Warman, especially, gave me her company, criticism, and moral support when I needed it most. My debt to my parents, and to my stepfather, is best left recorded (it cannot be expressed) in the dedication.

I

INTRODUCTION

ONE

On Kennan:
A Character Sketch

In Kennan's journalistic efforts . . . the scholar is continually vying with the misanthrope.

Ronald Steel

Kennan is an impressionist, a poet, not an
earthling.

Eugene V. Rostow

George F. Kennan, as he ruefully grants, is an anachronism.
Tall, slim, blue-eyed, gravely dignified, possessed of
Old Whig politics to go with his Old Whig demeanor, he is
nonetheless absorbed in—obsessed with, oppressed by—the
affairs of his own time. Diplomat, publicist, advisor to
presidents, he feels most at ease as historian, reconstructing
an earlier, somehow more familiar environment. He alter-
nates between recluse and elder statesman, with a deceptive
moderation of manner and speech. For all his careful control
and seeming detachment, Kennan has never divorced his

3

passion from his intellect. And yet the common passions of the politically engaged—power lust, an urge to be at the center of things, or even an abstract concern for justice—are almost altogether absent in Kennan. He is what the French call *sérieux*, genuinely burdened, as he has been for most of his professional life, by the conviction that American foreign policy, and American society generally, are suffering tragic flaws.

This vision is never far from Kennan's work, coloring every judgment he makes and prodding him, to his great discomfort, to an active role in public affairs. Richard Ullman, a longtime friend of Kennan's, calls him "a genuinely reluctant contributor to the policy debate" and suggests he would have been happier as a full-time historian.[1] Kennan himself, in a revealing passage, is wistful for literary and cultural pursuits. Describing an idyllic visit to the estate of Leo Tolstoi in 1952, Kennan mixes regret for paths not taken with an underlying sense of duty to the choices he has made: "I was permitted to feel close to a world to which, I always thought, I could really have belonged, had circumstances permitted—belonged much more naturally and wholeheartedly than to the world of politics and diplomacy into which Fate had thrust me. . . ."[2]

Fate, for Kennan, was and is a profound sense of horror at the stakes involved in international politics. In 1927, two years out of Princeton, he watched from Hamburg as Weimar Germany struggled to cope with the legacy of a world war; two decades later he returned to see the "sweeping devastation," the "stupendous, careless destruction of civilian life and of material values, built up laboriously by human hands over the course of centuries," that had

---

[1]Richard H. Ullman, "The 'Realities' of George F. Kennan," *Foreign Policy*, No. 28, Fall 1977, p. 140.

[2]George F. Kennan, *Memoirs, 1950-1963* [hereafter *Memoirs* II] (Boston: Little, Brown & Co., 1972), p. 130.

ensued at Weimar's failure.[3] The lessons he drew were many, but among them was what might be called the snowball theory of history: the idea that great issues—peace and war, prosperity and decline—rarely present themselves as such; that they come concealed in the workaday choices of people and governments; that they are, consequently, not well planned; that

> one thing leads to another. Every mistake is in a sense the product of all the mistakes that have gone before it, from which fact it derives a sort of cosmic forgiveness; and at the same time every mistake is in a sense the determinant of all the mistakes of the future, from which it derives a sort of cosmic unforgiveableness. Our action in the field of foreign policy is cumulative.[4]

With this view of human events, it was impossible from the start for Kennan to remain aloof. He was too highly strung, too overwhelmed with the predicament of nations, too sensitive to larger forces, too impressed with the accuracy of his own analysis, to keep his views to himself. As a junior foreign service officer, a senior diplomat, and a semipublic figure after retirement from government, Kennan would never resist for long the drive to unburden himself of what were most often profound disagreements with the official line of thinking. He began his career plucking earnestly at the sleeves of his superiors and is closing it with exhortations in the public prints. In between he advised presidents from FDR to Kennedy. How, under the circumstances, he could ever have sequestered himself in pursuit of the arts and letters—in what conceivable world he could have been content to indulge his aesthetic preference for privacy and scholarship—is hard to imagine. For it was

---

[3] George F. Kennan, *Memoirs, 1925-1950* [hereafter *Memoirs* I] (Boston: Little, Brown & Co., 1967), pp. 22–23, 434–37.

[4] George F. Kennan, *American Diplomacy: 1900–1950* (New York: New American Library, 1951), p. 47.

5

always "evident to me, as to every thinking person, that my world, and that of my children, was in serious danger. Was there then nothing I could do about it?"[5]

Still, though he is drawn by conscience into public life, Kennan is also deeply ill at ease in his society and his time. Forever being likened to Henry Adams,[6] he feels revulsion at every form of ugliness, bad taste, and disrespect for tradition. He is fond of citing Burke and Gibbon. Moreover, Kennan somehow feels an obligation to set a personal example of civility and moderation. As he told George Urban in his famous *Encounter* interview of 1975, ". . . I deeply believe that kindliness and generosity in our personal behavior, and a refusal to be beastly to others even by way of reaction, are both moral and pragmatic qualities of the highest order." This conviction flows not merely from gentlemanliness, but also from the world view of a self-described "inveterate elitist":

> One has to distinguish between individual dispositions. There is always a small minority—perhaps 10 or 15%—who have values, insights, sensitivity far greater than the mass of their fellow beings, and it is very important how this pattern-setting minority behave. Beyond that, you have the mass of the people, perhaps 70%, who are the common run of humanity with their normal strengths and weaknesses. . . . At the far end of the spectrum you find a minority of villains and felons with whom society has to deal as best it can.[7]

And while all this may seem an oddly chosen starting point for a discussion of foreign affairs, much of Kennan's personal style has its roots in a hierarchical, essentially

---

[5] Kennan, *Memoirs* II, p. 13.

[6] See, for example, Paul Seabury, "George Kennan vs. Mr. 'X': The Great Container Springs a Leak," *The New Republic*, December 16, 1981, p. 17.

[7] George F. Kennan and George Urban, "A Conversation," reprinted in Kennan et al., *Encounters with Kennan: The Great Debate* (London: Frank Cross and Company Limited, 1979), pp. 10, 12.

eighteenth-century vision of society. That style, and that vision, will have great importance for his political philosophy.

For within the gentleman-scholar, wrestling quietly with his own peculiar form of *Unbehagen* at twentieth-century America, there dwells an almost cantankerous man—the sort whose peace of mind is ruined regularly by the incompetence, as he sees it, of the men and women in power. George Kennan does not fully sympathize with or understand democracy, and, what is more important here, he does not always act or argue as if he is part of one. Of this he is forthrightly aware: "A stricter sense of administrative logic; a greater fastidiousness about the allotment of tasks and responsibilities . . . a preference for hierarchy and authority over compromise and manipulation; and a distaste amounting almost to horror for the chaotic disorder of the American political process: all these affected my view of political Washington. . . . It was a matter of temperament." In contrast to the "intolerable corruption" of domestic politics, Kennan inclines to the rather "purer" function of civil service and career diplomacy. Whenever he watched politics intrude on policy, Kennan writes, "I felt as I can imagine the surgeon might feel if told to deflect the knife and make the cut in a different and unsuitable place because he might look better, so doing, to people in the seats of the theater."[8]

The metaphor of the surgeon is apt in several ways. It suggests, for one thing, a truly disinterested performer of public duty, concerned only to serve the national weal. It suggests that there are objectively right and wrong ("suitable" and "unsuitable") ways of going about the task. And it suggests that the possibilities for useful argument as between the surgeon and the layman—the professional and the uninitiate—are limited. All these are basic to Kennan's intellectual temperament.

---

[8]Kennan, *Memoirs* II, pp. 322, 323.

There is an unfortunate tendency in Kennan's writings to equate "understanding" of his position with agreement. His opponents in argument, that is, do not disagree with but fail to grasp the reality of what he is saying.[9] This has, to Kennan's misfortune, often been true. But the frequent truth of it does not fully explain Kennan's persistent flirtation with the idea that duty, dedication, sensitivity, reason, and integrity, applied in sensible proportions, will lead to a single sound conclusion—Kennan's—in most issues of public policy. Kennan's critics often accuse him of issuing *ex cathedra* pronouncements, or behaving as if he thinks himself a judge rather than as a party to a dispute, and there is some truth to the charge.

On the other hand, Kennan's sometimes preachy style does not derive, as some critics suppose, from hubris. It is the product of a process of judgment that is more often intuitive than analytic—stemming, that is, not from premises and deductions but rather from a sort of panoramic apprehension of the forces at work in the world around him. Eugene Rostow sneers that Kennan is "an impressionist, a poet, not an earthling," a man whose mind "has never moved along mathematical lines, and never will." John Lewis Gaddis puts it more kindly, and much more reasonably, when he refers to Kennan's emphasis on "noncommunicable wisdom."[10] In his government years, Kennan never had patience for rigid simplifications and artificialities, preferring, on the basis of long experience and careful study, to try to gauge the imponderables. His intuitive vision, coupled with his facility for language, could translate into extraordinary eloquence; but if official opinion withstood the assault of his pen, as often happened, Kennan had little recourse in debate. He could not, after all, pass on his

---

[9]See, for example: *Memoirs* I, pp. 204, 417, 457; *Memoirs* II, pp. 161, 249, 288, 300.

[10]Eugene V. Rostow, "Searching for Kennan's Grand Design," *The Yale Law Journal*, June 1978; John Lewis Gaddis, *Strategies of Containment* (New York: Oxford University Press, 1982), p. 87.

experience and judgment themselves, but only their products. And yet, what first his superiors and later the reading public would want, in Dean Acheson's words, "was communicable wisdom, not mere conclusions, however soundly based in experience or intuition. . . ."[11]

Because Kennan believes himself (though in modesty he never quite says so) to be one of a select few sensitive realists, and because of his emphasis on the noncommunicable, he was destined to live a lonely intellectual existence for most of his career. Loneliness, in fact, is a theme that runs through both volumes of his *Memoirs*, from the awkwardness and isolation of Kennan's undergraduate days to his sad—almost pathetic—final departure from the career foreign service in 1953: "It occurred to me, then, that one would normally, on completion of twenty-seven years of service with a great organization, say goodbye to someone before leaving it. . . . I cast around, in my mind's eye. . . . At first I was unable to think of anyone."[12]

George Urban, in the opening observation of his exchange with Kennan, drew attention to this theme, citing a cluster of broadly synonymous expressions:

> They all have to do with your personal anguish at seeing the world, and especially the contemporary world, governed by myopia, ignorance, and folly; and they express your loneliness and helplessness in the face of so much, as you see it, avoidable evil. You are "totally caught . . . totally helpless . . . in black despair . . . horrified . . . lonely . . . extremely lonely . . . afflicted by loneliness . . . profoundly depressed . . . vulnerable." You have a "foreknowledge of disaster"; you raise "anguished objections"; you feel "tossed" into some "impossible position between two worlds"; and

---

[11]Dean Acheson, *Present at the Creation: My Years in the State Department* (New York: W.W. Norton & Co., 1969), p. 348.

[12]Kennan, *Memoirs* II, p. 188.

you are overcome by a sense of the enormity of responsibility and of our inadequacy to it.[13]

Such is Kennan's travail, a burden assumed quite deliberately. He has never had the iconoclast's taste for heresy—has, in fact, always been appalled when his dissents drew controversy down about him—but dissent he does. One detects the faint impression of Galileo's final testimony in Kennan's self-portrait: stoutly insistent, in the face of orthodoxy, "And yet, it moves."

As early as 1944, he was mapping his place in current affairs with, to crib a favorite Kennan phrase, a sigh and a sinking of the heart:

> The apprehension of what is valid in the Russian world is unsettling and displeasing to the American mind. He who would undertake this apprehension will not find his satisfaction in the achievement of anything practical for his people, still less in any official or public appreciation for his efforts. The best he can look forward to is the lonely pleasure of one who stands at long last on a chilly and inhospitable mountaintop where few have been before, where few can follow, and where few will consent to believe that he has been.[14]

To complete the mountaintop image, a skeptic might jibe, Kennan should have inscribed his *Memoirs* on tablets of stone. On the other hand, a man must be excused for taking some solace in the solitude of his views when, in the end, he fears so much may be lost for their lack of currency.

*   *   *

For all the talk of solitude, the portrait of Kennan as hapless dissident could easily be overdrawn. As a high-level

---

[13]Kennan and Urban, "A Conversation," p. 1.

[14]George F. Kennan, *Russia — Seven Years Later*, reprinted as appendix, *Memoirs* I, pp. 530–31.

planner in the State Department between 1946 and 1948, Kennan enjoyed a celebrity in Washington that few before or after him have known. It would have intoxicated another man, but Kennan was always more nearly bewildered by the sensation he created. The gratification of stardom was outweighed, characteristically, by anxiety lest he be misunderstood.

Beginning with his famous "long telegram" of 1946 and ending sometime before the signing of the Atlantic Pact in 1949, George Kennan was at the height of his influence in the foreign policy establishment. He had already enjoyed a meteoric flight (by State Department standards) through the ranks of the career foreign service, rising to second-in-command at the Moscow embassy by 1943. He had been trying for years to impress upon official Washington his views on the very limited potential of relations with the Soviet Union. By 1946, frustrated at their failures, FDR's advisors finally were ready to hear what Kennan had to say. The result was the "long telegram," some 8,000 words ("an outrageous encumberment of the telegraphic process") of Kennan's accumulated wisdom on Russia, America, Europe, and the postwar balance of power.[15] It created a sensation. The rest is well known: Kennan was recalled to Washington, lectured prolifically, wrote the "X-Article" advocating "containment" for *Foreign Affairs*, became George Marshall's Director of Policy Planning, played a leading role in drafting the Marshall Plan—and then, unaccountably but inexorably, faded away. By 1949, Kennan had asked to retire, and though he had brief stints ahead of him as ambassador in Moscow and Belgrade—what should have been the crown of his career—he would never again carry real weight in the department.

Actually, it is unclear how much weight he ever carried. Accounts diverge on exactly what influence Kennan wielded

---

[15]Kennan, *Memoirs* I, p. 294. For excerpts from the telegram, see pp. 547–59. The full text is on pages 696–709 of *Foreign Relations of the United States: 1946* [hereafter *FR*], Volume VI (Washington: Government Printing Office, 1969).

at his peak. Henry Kissinger writes that Kennan "came as close to authoring the diplomatic doctrine of his era as any diplomat in our history."[16] Kennan himself, typically, is a great deal more modest, asserting that he "made only a faint and wholly inadequate impression on official Washington."[17] John Lewis Gaddis, who has done the only thorough study of the period with access to Kennan's private papers and other important archival materials, comes down in the middle:

> To insist that Kennan's thinking either shaped or reflected that of the administration would be to oversimplify, for in fact it did both. Kennan himself acknowledges having played a decisive role in certain areas. . . . But Kennan's overall strategic concept . . . did not emerge fully formed in 1947; it was as much a rationalization for (and, at times, a critique of) what the administration did during the next three years as it was an impetus to those actions.[18]

Whatever the relations of cause and effect, the period between 1946 and 1948 was the only time in Kennan's long career when, from his perspective, the great political seesaw of American foreign policy was in anything close to balance. Before 1946, he saw everything tilted leftward—with talk of Uncle Joe Stalin and rosy predictions of Soviet–American harmony—and he struggled mightily to shift the weight of opinion to the right. After 1948, the seesaw did skew rightward—with what Kennan sees as an oversimplified and overmilitarized view of the Soviet problem—and he has spent more than three decades since tugging vainly to bring it level once again.[19] In his long-suffering tilt against the tilt, Kennan has not suffered a lack of critics. Branded cynical in

---

[16] Henry Kissinger, *White House Years* (Boston: Little, Brown & Co., 1979), p. 135.

[17] Kennan, *Memoirs I*, p. 403.

[18] Gaddis, *Strategies of Containment*, pp. 54–55.

[19] Kennan, *Memoirs I*, p. 134.

his early days, he has long felt vindicated in those worried warnings against too much intimacy with Moscow. Now, when he is charged with being soft on Communism, Kennan can point out that he is "one of the few Americans who have had the distinction of being thrown out of Stalin's Russia on charges of being too anti-Soviet."[20]

Oddly, though he aspires to influence in the policy process, Kennan gives the impression of a man who has been buffeted about in his career by forces he cannot fully understand. He pronounces himself mystified as to "why so much attention was paid in certain instances . . . to what I had to say, and so little in others."[21] Certainly, he has had very little control, or even warning, of the effect his words would create. He never imagined, for instance, the international furor that would ensue upon delivery of his Reith lectures over British Broadcasting Corporation radio in 1957, or that he would become a hero of the left with his Einstein Award speech of 1981. But here I get ahead of myself.

Kennan, in his own view, had only very rarely helped guide official decisionmaking. He reflected on this, with a touch of the bittersweet, in a parting verse penned for the Planning Staff in 1950:

> . . . Unaided, unencouraged to pursue
> The rarer bloom, the deeper hue,
> The choicer fragrance—these to glean
> And, having gleaned, to synthesize
> And long in deepest reticence to hide . . .
> Until some distant day—perhaps—permitted,
> Anonymous and unidentified,
> The Great White Queen
>   at last
>   to fertilize. . . .[22]

---

[20]Kennan, "The Ethics of Anti-Communism," *University: A Princeton Quarterly*, No. 24, Spring 1965, p. 3.

[21]Kennan, *Memoirs I*, p. 403.

[22]Quoted in ibid., p. 469.

Kennan's disdain for politics, even bureaucratic maneuvering, always stood between his ideas, however fertile, and the object of his passion. He spent his early days "writing without an audience" ("for the drawer," as Russians say) and found his later role, under Dean Acheson after George Marshall had stepped down as Secretary of State, reduced to that of a "court jester, expected to enliven discussion, privileged to say the shocking things . . . but not to be taken fully seriously. . . ."[23] Acheson, in a comment that would be typical of Kennan's superiors, said Kennan "mingled flashes of prophetic insight [with] suggestions . . . of total impracticality."[24]

All this grew rather discouraging. "I was inclined to wonder," Kennan wrote in his diary of July 12, 1950, "whether the day had not passed when the government had use for the qualities of persons like [me]—for the effort at cool and rational analysis in the unfirm substance of the imponderables. . . ."[25] From this thought came despair, and then a plan. "Never before," Kennan wrote on August 14, 1950,

> has there been such utter confusion in the public mind with respect to US foreign policy. The president doesn't understand it; Congress doesn't understand it; nor does the public, nor does the press. . . . Only the diplomatic historian, working from the leisure and detachment of a later day, will be able to unravel this incredible tangle and to reveal the true aspect of the various factors and issues involved. *And that is why, as it seems to me, no one in my position can contribute very much more . . . unless he first turns historian, earns public confidence and respect through the study of an earlier day, and then gradually carries the public up to a clear and comprehensive view of the occurrences of these recent years.*[26]

---

[23]Ibid., pp. 93, 230–31, 427.
[24]Acheson, *Present at the Creation*, pp. 147–48.
[25]Quoted in *Memoirs* I, p. 499.
[26]Quoted in ibid., p. 500 [emphasis added].

This plan was notable for its nearly perfect inverse relationship to Kennan's unfolding career. Far from beginning with the past and working his way up to the present, Kennan was dragged immediately into the fray of current affairs, becoming, as he pegged himself, "a semi-historian and a semi-commentator."[27] If there was any chronological progression, in fact, it dropped from the present into the past, for his first book was about contemporary diplomacy, and his most recent work is a multivolume history of the pre-World-War-I Franco–Russian alliance.[28]

Along the way, Kennan has been impressively prolific—writing 17 books, nearly all of them later excerpted in newspapers and magazines; 15 introductions, chapters, or afterwords in books by other authors; perhaps 75 articles; 13 book reviews; 14 published statements before Congress; some 30 letters to the editor; at least 45 published speeches; 18 published interviews; and well over 200 unpublished lectures. Add to that his meticulous, uncompromisingly literate diaries and untold personal correspondence. Surely few men or women in this century have written so much of importance.[29]

Nor has Kennan lacked for literary recognition, although he never earned a formal Ph.D. (At least 18 institutions of higher learning—including Princeton, Harvard, Yale, Oxford, Brandeis, Michigan, Kenyon, Notre Dame, and Duke—have corrected this anomaly by presenting him with honorary doctorates.) His honors include two Pulitzer Prizes, a Bancroft Prize, a National Book Award, a Benjamin Franklin Award—and Princeton's Woodrow Wilson Award, the highest honor it grants to an undergraduate alumnus.

---

[27]Kennan, *Memoirs* II, p. 13.

[28]Only the first volume—*The Decline of Bismarck's European Order* (Princeton: Princeton University Press, 1979)—has seen print. The second volume's manuscript is now nearing completion.

[29]See "Bibliography of Published Writings and Unpublished Addresses and Lectures of George Frost Kennan," private manuscript, 1974, as amended. It runs to 79 pages itself.

Still, far from escaping the alienation that had dogged him in his government years, Kennan continued to drag it around in his second career as a scholar–*philosophe*. Satisfaction in his public pursuits would remain a will-o'-the-wisp all his life, in part, perhaps, because he was so profoundly ambivalent about his own purposes. He wished to influence public opinion, true, but when his Reith lectures struck a nerve—when they "attracted vastly more interest and stimulated vastly more controversy" in America and Europe than anything the President or Secretary of State had said[30]—Kennan was merely miserable:

> [T]he torrents of publicity, the hundreds of comments, the unjust attacks, the telling criticisms—all this came to constitute for me, in the most literal sense of the term, a traumatic experience. I was utterly appalled and unsettled by the turmoil I had unleashed.[31]

Yet the deeper cause of Kennan's discomfort was not controversy but the inescapable fact that his ideas had not generated widespread support. "Aware of that failure," Kennan writes, "I came away from [the Reith lectures] in a state which I can only describe as one of intellectual brokenheartedness. . . ." He turned to "pursuit of history, the common refuge of those who find themselves helpless in the face of the present."[32] Thus was Kennan's circle squared. He had left government for history, that he might influence the present; now he turned to the past again because his own time had grown too painful and too strange.

Closing the second volume of the *Memoirs*, Kennan observed in 1972 that the account of his life's work "lends

---

[30]Joseph Alsop, *Chicago Sun Times*, quoted in Kennan, *Memoirs* II, p. 236.
[31]Ibid., p. 255.
[32]Ibid., p. 261.

itself . . . to a depressing interpretation."[33] He need hardly
have mentioned it. As he sees the world now, the danger is if
anything greater and the response if anything less resolute
than when he entered public life. He has attracted, in his
own mind, "no great body of followers." The Urban
interview and the book that followed it—*The Cloud of
Danger*—are the work of a man who is weary and nearly
without hope. At the dusk of his career, George Kennan
says: "I can not see the end of it all."[34]

*   *   *

One may wonder what could have brought Kennan to
such a pass, what gap between hope and life has left him so
bleak. For that I must turn back to his philosophy, which is,
after all, the point of this book.

Walter Lippmann once wrote that a "man's philosophy is
his autobiography; you may read in it the story of his conflict
with life."[35] With Kennan it works the other way around:

> I have made no attempt to summarize the outlook to
> which these various experiences led. To do that would
> be to depart entirely from the character of memoirs and
> to undertake a treatise on the philosophy of poli-
> tics. . . . Some of this philosophy will, I trust, shine
> through the accounts of episodes now long past. . . .[36]

Kennan's autobiography, in other words, is his philosophy,
for he steadfastly refuses to state his views systematically.
Notwithstanding occasional feints in the direction of
"expressing . . . something that might be called a personal

---

[33]Ibid., p. 319.

[34]Kennan and Urban, "A Conversation," p. 2.

[35]Walter Lippmann, in *The New Republic*, July 17, 1915; quoted in
Ronald Steel, *Walter Lippmann and the American Century* (Boston: Little,
Brown & Co., 1980), p. ix.

[36]Kennan, *Memoirs* II, pp. vii–viii.

philosophy of foreign policy," or of laying a "firm theoretical groundwork,"[37] Kennan has all his professional life scorned doctrines, formulas, and pretensions to universal truth.

If, then, in the chapters to follow, I will be trying to cut and paste Kennan's biography into philosophy, I should first make clear why the man himself has never had any taste for the project.

Kennan's particularism (if I can call it that) flows, first, from a conviction that seems odd in a prose stylist of his stature: he simply does not believe that words are capable of expressing universals or of conveying the complexity of real life. "I had no confidence," he writes of his government days, "in the ability of men to define hypothetically in any useful way, by means of general and legal phraseology, future situations which no one could really imagine or envisage."[38] It is, he says, "a world of relative and unstable values." Policy planners should "put away childish things; and among these childish things the first to go, in my opinion, should be . . . the search for absolutes in world affairs. . . ."[39]

Now, no one really disputes these points, and another writer might have gone on to conclude merely that one should be wary of absolutes, take account of exceptions, and look for second-best solutions. Kennan seems to conclude much more strongly that systematic expression is not worth attempting at all. To understand him here requires a look beyond the truism that the world is complicated, since that point does, after all, become pedantic eventually.

Sweeping doctrines are not only oversimplified, in Kennan's view, but hopeless. Policy planners have a hard enough time concentrating on the subtlety and evanescence

---

[37]George F. Kennan, *Realities of American Foreign Policy* (New York: W. W. Norton & Company, Inc., 1966) [first published 1954 by Princeton University Press], p. 3; Kennan, *Memoirs* I, p. 468.

[38]Kennan, *Memoirs* I, p. 408.

[39]George F. Kennan, *Russia and the West under Lenin and Stalin* (Boston: Little, Brown & Co., 1960), p. 397.

of international politics when they are not tempted by official formulas. The mere presence of a stated doctrine, because it tends to guide bureaucracies, therefore "shackles and distorts the process of decision-taking. It causes questions to be decided on the basis of criteria only partially relevant or not relevant at all. It tends to exclude at many points the discrimination of judgment and the prudence of language requisite to the successful conduct of the affairs of a great power."[40]

The final strand of Kennan's particularism goes one step further. Not only do universal principles botch up sensible planning, they can actively do harm in themselves. "I suppose I belong to that, for Marxists, most objectionable class of people who are neither Marxists nor anti-Marxists but live outside the entire conceptual framework of both," Kennan said at the close of the Urban interview. "I have seen too much beastliness committed in the name of messianic ideas. . . ."[41] Kennan puts his emphasis on means, not ends:

> Humanity divides . . . between those who, in their political philosophy, place the emphasis on order and those who place it on justice. I belong in the first of those categories. Human justice is always imperfect. The laws on which it bases itself are always to some extent unjust. These laws have therefore only a relative value; and it is only relative benefits that can be expected from the effort to improve them. But the good order of society is something tangible and solid. There is little that can be done about men's motives; but if men can be restrained in their behavior, something is accomplished. . . . The benefit of the doubt should lie, therefore, with the forces of order, not with the world-improvers.[42]

---

[40]Kennan, *Memoirs* I, p. 324.

[41]Kennan and Urban, "A Conversation," p. 82.

[42]George F. Kennan et al., *Democracy and the Student Left* (Boston: Little, Brown & Co., 1968), pp. 170–71. See also Kennan and Urban, "A Conversation," pp. 9, 27–29; Kennan, *Memoirs* I, pp. 199, 290.

Only methods—as opposed to purposes—are real, Kennan believes, and thus purposes are irrelevant as long as the methods are moderate and civil.

There is much that could be debated on all these points, and I will dispute some of them with Kennan in chapters to come. What is important here is to take note that in personal life, domestic politics, and foreign affairs alike, Kennan stresses means over ends, tactics over strategy, execution over concept. Before he can do so, it seems to me, Kennan must have in mind *some* idea of how the world works and how things ought to be done within it. That idea, in the argot of political scientists, is known as descriptive and normative theory. Whether he likes it or not, Kennan has a system.

Finally, for now, a word about consistency. Systems are sometimes consistent, sometimes not, usually a bit of both. For the particularist like Kennan, at any rate, inconsistency should not be a cardinal sin. Yet he has repeatedly laid claim to philosophical consistency in interviews and published writings.[43] His critics, on the other hand, rarely fail to latch on to any number of alleged contradictions—and a favorite form of Kennan-bashing is to chide Kennan-the-dove with Kennan-the-hawk's words, or vice versa.[44] That sort of argument will certainly not be settled here, nor probably by the end of this book. Suffice it for the moment to say that the charges of contradiction tend to be made rather loosely. With that, my capacity for general conclusions is exhausted. If I am to get any farther, it will have to be by returning—no doubt, to Kennan's great relief—to the particulars.

---

[43]In Marilyn Berger, "An Appeal for Thought," *The New York Times Magazine*, May 7, 1978, Kennan was asked: "But you feel your views have been consistent?" He replied: "Well, they have, to my mind." See also Kennan and Urban, "A Conversation," p. 63; and, in the same volume, George F. Kennan, "A Last Warning: Reply to My Critics," p. 161.

[44]See, for example, Michael Novak, "George X. Kennan versus George Y. Kennan," *The Washington Star*, December 29, 1977; Edward N. Luttwak, "The Strange Case of George F. Kennan: From Containment to Isolationism," *Commentary*, November 1977; Rostow, "Searching for Kennan's Grand Design"; Leopold Labedz, "The Two Minds of George Kennan: How to Un-Learn from Experience," *Encounter*, April, 1978; Seabury, "George Kennan vs. Mr. 'X'."

II

THE PURPOSES
OF POWER

TWO

On Strategy and the National Interest

[Kennan has] a depth of strategic vision . . .
rarely found in harried bureaucracies.

John Lewis Gaddis

[What Kennan] knows about strategy could
be inscribed without too much congestion on
the back of a Green Shield stamp.

Lord Chalfont

Rarely can a man have been so persistently haunted by his
own words as George Kennan by "The Sources of Soviet
Conduct," which he published pseudonymously in 1947.[1]
No article in the history of *Foreign Affairs* has been so often
reprinted,[2] had such enduring currency, or, it may be safe to

---

[1] X [pseud. for George F. Kennan], "The Sources of Soviet Conduct,"
Foreign Affairs, July 1947, pp. 566–82.
[2] It has been reprinted or excerpted at least 39 times, by Kennan's
accounting ("Bibliography of Published Writings," pp. 15–18).

assert, attracted so peculiar a coalition of friends and foes. To get a full grasp of the anachronism of its continuing place in the foreign policy debate, one need only flip through the rest of the July, 1947, issue in which it appeared. There will be found a debate on the Munich crisis; a piece called "Putting the Nuremberg Law to Work"; and a discussion of "Self-Government in U.S. Territories"—including Alaska, Hawaii, and the Philippines. Yet Kennan's piece lives on.

The X-Article, so called because Kennan signed it "X" (*not* "Mr. X") in a doomed stab at anonymity, introduced the term "containment" to public discourse. It at once provoked a great uproar and much confusion, and it has dogged Kennan's footsteps ("like a faithful but unwanted and somewhat embarrassing animal") ever since.[3] That the article left some important questions unanswered is hardly surprising, since Kennan never dreamed it would be interpreted as a broad strategic plan for American power in the postwar period. But its elliptical quality and prominent role in debates on everything from the Marshall Plan to the Truman Doctrine have sparked, even three decades later, what John Lewis Gaddis calls "a kind of cottage industry" of continuing exegesis.[4]

In his own recent book, Gaddis was the first to use Kennan's private papers and off-the-record, now declassified, lectures at the National War College to place the X-Article within the larger context of Kennan's strategic thought as it developed from 1946 to 1949. This chapter, parts of which draw on Gaddis' work, adds to his analysis

---

[3]George F. Kennan, "Mr. X Reconsiders: A Current Assessment of Soviet-American Relations," in Kennan et al., *Encounters with Kennan*, p. 111.

[4]Gaddis, *Strategies of Containment*, p. 26. If it is an industry, Gaddis has helped it along considerably. In addition to his book, he wrote "Containment: A Reassessment," *Foreign Affairs*, July 1977, pp. 873–87. See also: Eduard Mark, "The Question of Containment: A Reply to John Lewis Gaddis," *Foreign Affairs*, January 1978, pp. 430–40; Charles Gati, "What Containment Meant," *Foreign Policy*, Summer 1972, pp. 22–40; C. Ben Wright, "Mr. 'X' and Containment," *Slavic Review*, March 1976, pp. 1–31.

and extends it to the present day. Following Kennan's distinction between ends and means,[5] I will limit discussion here (insofar as possible) to the objectives and broad strategy of American power, saving methods and tactics for Chapter 5.

I

Kennan believes, unabashedly, in a notion that has gone out of style in the past two or three decades: that there is a more or less objective national interest, and that ordinary mortals are equipped to discover it. The "national interest" underlies much of what Kennan has to say about strategy. Later in this discussion I will need to look at this concept more closely. For now I merely take note of it.

At least since the turn of the century, in Kennan's analysis, Americans have been aware "that our power had world-wide significance," and, moreover, "that we could be affected by events far afield; from that time on our interests were constantly involved in important ways with such events."[6] No longer could the United States take a detached view of foreign affairs, or bring to them "the concepts and methods of a small neutral nation," as it had done throughout the eighteenth and nineteenth centuries. That approach ("for which I must confess a certain nostalgia") would no longer suffice to preserve a stable world or protect American interests abroad.[7]

To Kennan's mind, power was at best a mixed blessing. When he spoke of it in public lectures in the first few years of his retirement from the Foreign Service, he seemed to be reminding himself as well as his listeners that there was no

---

[5]See Chapter 1.
[6]Kennan, *American Diplomacy*, foreword.
[7]Ibid., pp. 79–80; Kennan, *Realities of American Foreign Policy*, pp. 12–14.

going back to America's early years: "We cannot help wielding this power. It comes to us by virtue of our sheer size and strength, whether we wish it or not." And: "We have become . . . like a giant in a crowded room: we may wish to have nothing to do with the others, but everywhere we move we crowd someone or step on someone, and we have no choice but to recognize the resulting social obligation."[8] By this obligation, Kennan meant nothing in the way of a moral duty—he believed merely that the fact of American power should occasion some serious thought about its interests and objects.

No amount of international collaboration, he stressed, could substitute for a clear sense of purpose and resolve in the United States itself. In March, 1954, delivering the Stafford Little Lecture Series to a standing-room-only crowd in Princeton's Alexander Hall,[9] Kennan warned against leaning too heavily on the Atlantic Pact or on the newly formed United Nations:

> There is no use blinking the fact that we are a great nation, with nearly one-half of the world's wealth and a sizeable portion of its military power. This is a heavy responsibility. It rests squarely on us. We will not really evade it or spread it extensively by contriving always to appear in the company of an international majority. . . . I am merely urging that we try to preserve at all times a correct relationship between power and responsibility and that we do not attempt to involve in complicated international problems large numbers of countries whose interests may be only remotely affected by them, and who will be powerless to make any appreciable contribution to such remedies as it may be necessary to adopt.[10]

---

[8]Kennan, *Russia and the West*, p. 397; Kennan, *Realities of American Foreign Policy*, p. 104.

[9]Kennan, *Realities of American Foreign Policy*, preface to the Norton edition, 1966, p. vii. See also *The Daily Princetonian*, March 24 to April 1, 1954.

[10]Kennan, *Realities of American Foreign Policy*, p. 45.

This unyielding insistence on the recognition of power realities—of all "realities," in fact, as against theories, hopes, and ideals—would never be far from Kennan's thought.

Meanwhile, there was the matter of the national interest. What, exactly, should America do with its power?

Six years before the Little Lectures, Kennan had typed out, apparently for his private papers only, the nearest thing to a definition of the national interest he would ever write:

> The fundamental objectives of our foreign policy must always be:
>
> 1. to protect the security of the nation, by which is meant the continued ability of this country to pursue the development of its internal life without serious interference, or threat of interference, from foreign powers; and
> 2. to advance the welfare of its people, by promoting a world order in which this nation can make the maximum contribution to the peaceful and orderly development of other nations and derive maximum benefit from their experiences and abilities.[11]

This, Gaddis writes, was rather "bland and unexceptionable"; but, of course, it needed elaboration.[12]

Kennan gave the idea some philosophical underpinning before his attentive crowd in Alexander Hall. The conduct of foreign relations, he said, can have no objectives in and of itself. It is not "a purpose . . . . for a political society," but rather "one of the means by which some higher and more comprehensive purpose is pursued." Every society, Kennan argued, has had such an overarching purpose to justify its

---

[11]Draft paper, "Comments on the General Trend of U.S. Foreign Policy," August 20, 1948, *The George F. Kennan Papers* [hereafter *Kennan Papers*], Box 23, Seeley G. Mudd Library, Princeton University. Later in this paper, Kennan would outline, in similar numbered-point form, the possible measures of American power projection. See Chapter 5.

[12]Gaddis, *Strategies of Containment*, p. 27.

separate sovereignty—the promotion of dynasty, for instance, and the extension of its prestige and power; or the cultivation of national identity; or the application of a given social theory. This purpose may have been crude or vaguely formulated ("more felt than expressed"), but, Kennan said, "I suspect it has always been there." The national interest in foreign affairs, then, would flow logically from "whatever we consider to be the general objects of American society."[13]

Kennan, to this point, had developed his lecture quite systematically. He had a premise (that foreign policy is a means and not an end) and an argument from that premise (that the national interest would derive from the general objects of American society)—but now, maddeningly, his lecture left the ground and began to soar above the political landscape with an elusive grace that no doubt tempted the audience to overlook Kennan's failure ever to come in for a landing. Just on the verge, or so it seemed, of defining the national purpose—and then, presumably, going on to derive the objects of American foreign policy—Kennan began a slow digression that eventually amounted to a change of subject altogether.

This is how it worked. Kennan paused, reasonably, for some historical background, consulting the founding fathers on the purposes of American society. He came away with the familiar "natural rights" of life, liberty, and the pursuit of happiness, as well as "the right to hold property and to dispose over it." The state was not "the bearer of any concrete social program," though Kennan acknowledged that *laissez faire* had never been applied in its purest form. The upshot was that, in looking for principles of foreign

---

[13]Kennan, *Realities of American Foreign Policy*, pp. 4–6. In another lecture, Kennan said the national interest "is *not* a detached interest in our international environment pursued *for its own sake*, independent of our aspirations and problems here at home. It does not signify things we would like to see happen in the outside world primarily for the sake of the outside world. . . . It is the function of our duty to ourselves in our domestic problems." ("Lectures on Foreign Policy," *Illinois Law Review*, January–February 1951, p. 730. Emphasis in original.)

relations in the original vision of American society, "you came up with a policy very modest and very restrained." It had only two objects: first, to "protect the physical intactness of our national life from any external military or political intrusion" and, second, "to promote and protect" American citizens in their pursuit of private interests abroad. These objects called for a "very alert and vigorous and imaginative attention to the real sources of our national security," but nothing more.[14]

So far, so good. But at this point, Kennan became distracted by the contrast between realism and romanticism, between a clear-eyed view of power realities and a lofty aspiration to moral purpose. This is a contrast—a dichotomy, in Kennan's view—to which I will return in Chapter 3. What is important here is that Kennan never really came back to national purpose and national interest. And what is distressing about his failure to do so is that he clearly does not believe that the eighteenth-century conception of national interest is fully applicable to twentieth-century America.

This example of Kennan's elusiveness as a thinker illustrates the primary difficulty of criticizing his overall system of thought. True, Kennan never claims to be a theorist, and he has no obligation to write abstractly or methodically. And yet the reader has no choice but to attribute to him a certain coherence and method of analysis, simply in order to grasp, let alone to criticize, what he is saying. The danger is that the reader will *construct* a framework for Kennan instead of reconstructing it.

Whatever else Kennan believes about the national interest, he clearly seems to think it is easily, even objectively, discernible in application. He does not even think it necessary to assert this belief directly; he inserts it, almost parenthetically, into a discussion of legal–moralism. We should "have the modesty to admit," he writes, "that our own national interest is all that we are really capable of

---

[14]Ibid., pp. 6–13.

knowing and understanding. . . . "[15] For purposes of later discussion, it may be useful to note now that Kennan regards "national interest" as a descriptive, not a normative, concept. That is, he apparently does not believe the discovery of the national interest to entail a value judgment.

In any case, Kennan did finally allude again to the national interest in the last of his 1954 Little Lectures:

> In the first of these lectures I spoke of the original objects of American society and of the modest limited concepts of foreign policy that flowed from them. These concepts still appeal to me strongly. . . . But I must confess that I do not think that the original objects from which these concepts flowed are now fully adequate to the present nature of our society, to the significance of our position in the world, and to the responsibilities that rest upon us. I believe, in other words, that we must consciously enlarge the objects of our society. . . .

Here again, seemingly on the verge of spelling out what he meant, Kennan retreated, this time by means of extraordinarily general language: "we [should] make it our object so to conduct ourselves in our capacity as a member of the world community as to enhance the chances for the preservation of the values we cherish here at home."[16]

Why this evasiveness? The real impediment to fleshing out Kennan's vision of the national interest is his reluctance to deal with ends at all, as distinct from means. This reluctance is soundly rooted in a diplomat's pragmatic good sense, but it is not merely anti-Utopian: it so deeply permeates Kennan's thinking as to leave him almost constitutionally unable to write anything about goals in and of themselves. He often seems not to believe that objectives, detached from methods, even exist at all. In his *Memoirs*, Kennan wrote:

---

[15]Kennan, *American Diplomacy*, p. 88.
[16]Kennan, *Realities of American Foreign Policy*, pp. 102–3, 104.

Objectives were normally vainglorious, unreal, extravagant, even pathetic—little likely to be realized, scarcely to be taken seriously. . . . But methods were another matter. These were real. It was out of their immediate effects that the quality of life was really molded. In war as in peace I found myself concerned less with what people thought they were striving for than with the manner in which they strove for it.[17]

He never published his most radical formulation of this belief:

Some of us are inclined to feel that even in international affairs the observance of good *form* and good manners has probably done more in the end for civilized and peaceful living than all the moralizing about the *content* of human behavior. What is important, in other words, is not so much *what* is done as *how* it is done. And in this sense, good form in outward demeanor becomes more than a means to an end, more than a subsidiary attribute: it becomes a value in itself, with its own validity and its own effectiveness, and perhaps— human nature being what it is—the greatest value of them all.[18]

In 1951, Kennan did publish a similar, if slightly weaker, statement: "It is a question of the 'how' rather than the 'what.' This is not to say that we do not have an interest as a nation in what we do and *what* results stem from our action; but I would submit that we have a greater interest still, a primary interest, in *how* we do these things which we feel ourselves obliged to do or cannot keep from doing."[19]

---

[17]Kennan, *Memoirs* I, p. 199.

[18]Lecture, "Russian–American Relations," delivered February 20, 1947, at the University of Virginia, *Kennan Papers*, Box 16 [emphasis added on "form" and "content"].

[19]Kennan, "Lectures on Foreign Policy," [emphasis in original]. See also letter to Acheson in *Memoirs* II, p. 31; *Memoirs* I, p. 290; *Russia and the West*, pp. 146–47, 233.

From a ship's captain, such a what-versus-how philoso- phy, in its pure application, might prompt an announcement that the ship would henceforth have no particular destina- tion. It would continue to sail, but primarily at the behest of the wind and tides—and insofar as the captain exerted any control over its path, it would be mostly to avoid obvious hazards and bad weather. This sort of navigation might serve the interest of keeping the ship intact. It could not do much else.

And yet: Kennan did have some other interest in mind at the end of his Little Lectures. In other words, there was some other *what* implicit in his suggestion, quoted earlier, that we "so . . . conduct ourselves . . . as to enhance the chances for the preservation of the values we cherish here at home." I would argue there were two.

The first stems from Kennan's lifelong preoccupation with the predicament of modern societies. He worries about the abuse and destruction of natural resources, the erosion of traditional, civilized values, and the corruption of human- kind's inner vitality. These concerns suggest a national interest—in foreign as in domestic affairs—in moral and environmental regeneration.

The second, it seems safe to suppose, stems from the responsibilities that come with power: those obligations, in Kennan's view, to which I referred at the start of this section. This would suggest an interest in the preservation of world order. (Because of a confluence of ends and means in Kennan's thought, it is hard to tell whether international equilibrium is the one or the other. It is probably both.) By this is meant order writ large, not small. Kennan, in other words, would have America work toward a stable interna- tional environment, not "keep order" in the schoolyard sense.

These two purposes seem to be the most that can be plausibly gleaned from Kennan's sparse talk of objectives. And even these two derive from the irreducible interests Kennan set forth in 1948. To go deeper into Kennan's thought will call, then, for a shift from the "what" to the "how"—from the objectives of national security and a congenial international environment to Kennan's broad strategy for achieving them.

II

Preeminent among all the realities of George Kennan, the reality-in-chief, is that of power relationships. Well before the "long telegram" launched him to prominence in the biggest strategic issue of the day, Kennan had been preoccupied with power. In 1946, as "deputy for foreign affairs" at the newly established National War College, Kennan helped found the discipline that would come to be known as national security studies. Along the way he formed ideas on power relationships that would be "basic to my views on American foreign policy ever since."[20]

Kennan began writing about national security at a time when the postwar international order was only just taking shape. The Potsdam and Yalta conferences were yesterday's news: Europe—East and West—was exhausted and in economic ruin; the United Nations was not yet two years old; the final partition of Germany was still to come; and the Soviet Union had only recently started looking like an implacable foe. There were few familiar reference points for those accustomed to the prewar order, and there was no clear consensus in the foreign policy establishment about what the future would bring.

With his usual penchant for synthesis, Kennan wrote that American security in the postwar period could be sought in two ways. One of them he called the "universalistic" approach—which, he wrote, was illusory and doomed to failure. Universalism would try to hide the "ugly realities" of international life ("the power aspirations, the national

---

[20]Kennan, *Memoirs* I, pp. 298, 306, 309.

prejudices, the irrational hatreds and jealousies") behind "standard rules of behavior . . . [and] the protecting curtain of legal restraint." It would lean heavily on multilateral organizations such as the United Nations; it would seek harmony in world affairs; and it would try in vain to rule military conflict out of international life. Kennan's alternative he called the "particularized" approach, which "considers that the thirst for power is still dominant among so many peoples that it cannot be assuaged or controlled by anything but counter-force." The particularized approach would require vigorous unilateral action by the United States, calling for alliances only where there was "real community of interest and outlook."[21]

Kennan's preference for particularism had its roots in three basic assumptions about the character of international life.

First, the balance of power was and would continue to be the only glue binding any international structure. In 1944, on hearing the first reports of the talks at Dumbarton Oaks, Kennan wrote: "An international organization for preservation of the peace and security cannot take the place of a well-conceived and realistic foreign policy. The more we ignore politics in our absorption with the erection of a legalistic system for the preservation of the status quo, the sooner and the more violently that system will be broken to pieces under the realities of international life." Exactly that had happened to the Holy Alliance and the League Nations, Kennan argued.[22]

Second, conflict and change were the very essence of international life, and no status quo, however realistically

---

[21]PPS/23, "Review of Current Trends: U.S. Foreign Policy," February 24, 1948, *FR: 1948*, I, pp. 526–27, quoted in Gaddis, *Strategies of Containment*, pp. 27–28.

[22]Private memorandum, August 14, 1944, quoted in *Memoirs* I, p. 218. In *Russia, the Atom and the West*, p. 27, he wrote: "No international organization can be stronger than the structure of relationships among the Great Powers that underlies it. . . ." See also *American Diplomacy*, p. 41; *Russia and the West*, p. 120.

conceived, could last intact forever. In relations among sovereign states, there is "nothing final in point of time, nothing not vulnerable to the law of change. . . ." The task of international politics, then, would be "not to inhibit change but to find means to permit change to proceed without repeatedly shaking the peace of the world." Any system imposed on international life, if it harbored hopes of surviving over the long term, would have to be "sufficiently subtle, sufficiently pliable, to adjust [itself] to constant change in the interests and power of the various countries involved."[23]

Third, there could be no guarantee that such change would proceed always by peaceful means—nor that peace would always be in the best interests of the United States. The very idea of a balance of power suggested dynamic tension—or, in other words, a latent violence. There might well be times when, for the sake of preserving the balance, that violence would come to the surface.

> Unpleasant as this may be, we may have to face up to the fact that there may be instances where violence somewhere in the world on a limited scale is more desirable than the alternatives, because those alternatives would be [eventual] global wars in which we ourselves would be involved, in which no one would win, and in which all civilization would be dragged down. I think we have to face the fact that there may be arrangements of peace less acceptable to the security of this country than isolated recurrences of violence.

Objecting, then, to the promise of permanent peace, Kennan held up a new goal: "Peace if possible, and insofar as it effects our interest."[24]

---

[23]Kennan, *Russia and the West*, p. 398; *Realities of American Foreign Policy*, p. 36; memorandum, August 4, 1944, quoted in *Memoirs* I, p. 218.
[24]National War College lecture, "Where Are We Today?" December 21, 1948: NWC lecture, "What Is Policy?" December 18, 1947, *Kennan Papers*, Box 17.

The tenor of these assumptions was such as to suggest that America, as the most powerful nation in the postwar order, would have a preeminent role in the maintenance of the balance of power. Indeed, in the X-Article for *Foreign Affairs*, Kennan appeared to advocate a virtually unlimited scope of responsibility for American power. In the article's best-known passages, Kennan called for "the adroit and vigilant application of counter-force at a series of constantly shifting geographical and political points," or, again, "at every point where they [the Russians] show signs of encroaching upon the interests of a peaceful and stable world."[25] Many critics have pointed out that this sounds worlds apart from some of Kennan's most recent work, in which he describes himself, with some qualification, as an "isolationist" and calls for the pruning and paring of American commitments around the world.[26]

If there has been a change in Kennan's thinking, and there undoubtedly has, it has not been quite as dramatic as it appears. For Kennan's essential views on power relationships have changed very little, if at all, from the immediate postwar period to the present. The changes have been almost entirely in what an economist would call the exogenous variables.

Even in 1947, the X-Article represented Kennan's overall strategy indifferently at best. Kennan's *post facto* assertion that this was the case is generally as little believed as it is well known,[27] and yet even a cursory acquaintance with the

---

[25][Kennan], "The Sources of Soviet Conduct," pp. 576, 581.

[26]Urban and Kennan, "A Conversation," p. 19; see also Kennan, *The Cloud of Danger: Current Realities of American Foreign Policy* (Boston: Little, Brown & Co., 1977). In a 1975 interview with Eric Severeid, Kennan said, "I think we couldn't lose anything at all by cutting a whole series of unsound commitments." (Severeid and Kennan, "A Conversation with George Kennan," *Vital History Cassettes*, Encyclopedia Americana/CBS News Audio Resource Library, 1975.)

[27]Kennan, *Memoirs* I, Chapter 15, pp. 354–67. For skeptical reactions, see: Eduard Mark, "What Kind of Containment?" in Thomas G. Paterson, ed., *Containment and the Cold War* (Reading, Mass.: Addison-Wesley Publishing Company, 1973); Wright, "Mr. 'X' and Containment."

Kennan Papers, as Gaddis first demonstrated, lends sub-stantial support to Kennan's claim.

Far from urging a policy of around-the-world responsi-bility for American power, as many readers believed and Walter Lippmann charged so zealously,[28] Kennan neither wished America to bear the full burden of the balance of power nor believed that all geographical areas were of equal importance in the balance. In fact, Kennan's lectures at the National War College and his private notes of the same period make plain that he hoped to share the burden among America's allies and had a clear sense that, even with such an alliance, limited resources would require that American planners establish a hierarchy of interests around the globe.

How Kennan contrived to create such a colossal misim-pression of his views in the X-Article has yet to be fully explained. Part of the answer lies in sloppy drafting—and in a later chapter I will return to that point in discussing the controversial question of what Kennan meant by "counter-force." Part of it lies in the undoubted fact that Kennan never meant the X-Article primarily as a programmatic discussion of American power: well over nine-tenths of it, after all, was devoted to describing political culture in the Soviet Union. Part of the confusion also lies in a combination of, first, Kennan's general dislike of responding to criticism and, second, his promotion, in the interim between submission and publication of the article, to a policy-level position from which he was not encouraged to speak his mind publicly. Still another part lies in the association in the public mind between Kennan's article and such contemporary govern-ment policies as the Truman Doctrine, with which Kennan had serious differences.

Fortunately, Kennan's actual views at the time are rather less mysterious than the process by which they came to be distorted.

---

[28]Walter Lippmann, *The Cold War: A Study in U.S. Foreign Policy* (New York: Harper & Brothers Publishers, 1947). See also Steel, *Walter Lippmann and the American Century*, pp. 443–46.

First and foremost, national security could be preserved only by the maintenance of equilibrium in the international order. For this the United States would need help: "We cannot unilaterally hold the world in balance. We may not like allies—but we've got to have them."[29] And, moreover, equilibrium might call for sowing dissension in the enemy ranks:

> Our safety depends on our ability to establish a balance among the hostile or undependable forces of the world: To put them where necessary one against the other; to see that they spend in conflict with each other, if they must spend it at all, the intolerance and violence and fanatacism which might otherwise be directed against us, that they are thus compelled to cancel each other out and exhaust themselves in internecine conflict in order that the constructive forces, working for world stability, may continue to have the possibility of life.[30]

However accomplished, the maintenance of equilibrium was essential. Kennan would make this point more colorfully in a later discussion of the breakdown of equilibrium that had led to World War I:

> I sometimes wonder whether . . . a democracy is not uncomfortably similar to one of those prehistoric monsters with a body as long as this room and a brain the size of a pin: he lies there in his comfortable primeval mud and pays little attention to his environment; he is slow to wrath—in fact, you practically have to whack his tail off to make him aware that his interests are being disturbed; but, once he grasps this, he lays about him with such blind determination that he not only destroys his adversary but largely wrecks his native habitat. You wonder whether it would not have been wiser for him

---

[29]NWC lecture, "What Is Policy?" December 18, 1947, *Kennan Papers*, Box 17.

[30]NWC lecture, "Where Are We Today?" December 21, 1948, *Kennan Papers*, Box 17.

to have taken a little more interest in what was going on at an earlier date and to have seen whether he could not have prevented some of these situations from arising. . . .[31]

Considerations of the power balance and recognition that U.S. resources were limited, however, suggested that some nations and regions were more important than others to U.S. interests. "We must not hope to hold everything everywhere," Kennan told a War College audience in 1947, even as his X-Article was being read as arguing just that. "We must decide which areas are key areas and which are not, which ones we must hold to with all our strength and which we may yield tactically."[32]

By 1948, Kennan had developed an idea of specific areas which, taken together, would constitute "an irreducible minimum of national security," and in which the American objective would be "the maintenance of political regimes . . . at least favorable to the continued power and independence of our nation." His list included:

1. The nations and territories of the Atlantic community, which include Canada, Greenland and Iceland, Scandinavia, the British Isles, western Europe, the Iberian Peninsula, Morocco and the west coast of Africa down to the bulge, and the countries of South America from the bulge north;
2. The countries of the Mediterranean and the Middle East as far east as, and including, Iran; and
3. Japan and the Philippines.[33]

One month later, as Gaddis writes, Kennan had refined his irreducible minimum again, this time asserting that there

---

[31]Kennan, *American Diplomacy*, p. 59.

[32]NWC lecture, "What is Policy?" December 18, 1947, *Kennan Papers*, Box 17.

[33]Draft paper, "Comments on the General Trend of U.S. Foreign Policy," August 20, 1948, *Kennan Papers*, Box 23.

were "only five centers of industrial and military power in the world which are important to us from the standpoint of national security." This was a concept that would stay with Kennan for the rest of his career. In 1954, for instance, he told his Princeton audience:

> Our own North American community constitutes one such center of military–industrial strength. There are only four others in the world. They are all in the Northern Hemisphere. Two of them, England and Japan, lie off the shores of the Eurasian land mass and belong to the insular and maritime portion of the globe, of which we Americans are also a part. The other two have their seat in the interior of the Eurasian land mass. One of these last two is made up of Germany and the industrial regions immediately contiguous to Germany. . . . The other is represented by the Soviet Union proper. . . . [N]owhere outside these five areas can military–industrial strength be produced in this world today on what we might call the grand scale.[34]

One of these military–industrial centers—the Soviet Union—was in hostile hands; and so the principal task of American security would be to keep the others out of similarly unfriendly control.

Gaddis calls this notion of five vital power centers a plan for "strongpoint" as opposed to "perimeter" security.[35] It did not imply that the four non-Soviet power centers were the only interests of the United States, but they were by far the most important ones. "What he was saying," Gaddis writes, "was that of the varieties of power that existed on the international scene, industrial–military power was the most dangerous, and hence *primary* emphasis should be placed on

---

[34] NWC lecture, "Contemporary Problems of Foreign Policy," September 17, 1948, *Kennan Papers,* Box 17; *Realities of American Foreign Policy,* p. 64. See also *Memoirs* I, p. 359; Gaddis, *Strategies of Containment,* p. 30.
[35] Gaddis, *Strategies of Containment,* p. 58.

keeping it under control."[36] Kennan, of course, saw interests outside his chosen strongpoints: in a secure sphere of influence in the Western hemisphere, in access to raw materials, in strategic transportation and communication routes.

Interdependence, in fact, and the unhappy tendency of our strategic interests to have interests of their own, would always be a problem for Kennan—especially in recent years, when he has become more eager to limit American commitments. For there has been a certain ambivalence of purpose in Kennan's delimitation of strongpoints. On the one hand, he has usually spoken of such perimeter sketches as *minimum* strategic interests, thereby recognizing the possibility of other important interests. On the other hand, he has shown a growing desire to decide on the *sufficient* or even *maximum* strategic interests of the United States. He wants to draw a line, tell any potential adversary, in effect, "cross here at your peril" and then leave the rest of the globe primarily to its own devices.[37]

The motivation for this change properly belongs elsewhere in this book, but it is appropriate to mention here that any such attempt to define in final form the bounds of America's global fortress is likely to be either redundant or insufficient, depending on your belief about the existence of a serious threat to the national security. If it is held that there are no forces seriously hostile to American interests, then there is no obvious need for any strategic perimeter, minimum or maximum or otherwise. If, on the other hand, the possibility of serious hostility is acknowledged, then—as Kennan-the-pragmatist surely should concede—any attempt to delimit in advance the dispensable and the indispensable is probably futile. Changing circumstances and inter-

---

[36]Ibid., p. 31 [emphasis in original].
[37]See for example, *The Cloud of Danger*; Berger, "An Appeal for Thought"; "'X' Plus 25: Interview with George F. Kennan," *Foreign Policy*, No. 7, Summer 1972, pp. 17–18; Severeid interview.

dependencies, Kennan should be the first to maintain, may change the priorities of American interests.

Korea, for example, never appeared even on Kennan's broadest sketch of indispensable strongpoints in 1948. Japan, however, did. And in the circumstances of 1950, Kennan was among the earliest advocates "that we would have to react with all necessary force . . . to expel the North Korean forces from the southern half of the peninsula."[38] The strategic position of the United States might not be bound up directly with that of South Korea, but Japan's was, and with that in mind Kennan saw little choice but to intervene.

Most recently, Kennan has distinguished among interests, "serious" interests, and "vital" interests—the last of which, he suggests, are associated with avoiding "mortal damage to our national life in the physical sense."[39] Whatever can be said for such distinctions, to the extent they are designed to be rigid or categorical they fit in only very poorly with the strategic conception Kennan developed in his War College years. No set of categories, Kennan emphasized in that period, could be expected to suffice in describing the dynamics of a balance of power.

Kennan would be unlikely now to dispute this point if pressed. It is, moreover, possible to read his writings of the past three decades as being technically consistent on the question of geographical strongpoints—I say technically, in the sense that there are no outright contradictions. But there has clearly been a change of emphasis. The sources of that change I earlier called exogenous to his strategic thought: they consist partly in his altered viewpoint on Soviet global intentions, and partly in a profoundly more pessimistic evaluation now than in 1947 of the health of American society and of its capacity to combine consistency and vigor in foreign affairs. Concomitant with these changes in viewpoint have come changes in the relationships among

---

[38]Kennan, *Memoirs* I, p. 486.
[39]Kennan, *The Cloud of Danger*, pp. 80–81.

America, Russia, and the other world powers. It is to these relationships that I now turn.

III

Never once in a long career's writings on foreign policy, so far as I could discover, has George Kennan brought himself to pen the word "superpower." For all his long engagement in problems of Soviet–American relations, Kennan has always sought a return to the sort of multipolar balance that flourished before World War I. He is far more at home with Great Powers than superpowers, and much of his thought on strategy has always turned on the prospect of restoring power centers in Europe and Asia to a place in the balance that corresponds to their "historical, economic, cultural, and demographic realities."[40]

Kennan's distaste for bipolarity should not be read as an abstract preference for anything like egalitarianism in politics among nations. In 1951, for instance, he wrote that the great disparities in industrial–military potentials and the fractious nature of coalitions together suggested a "law of diminishing returns" that made it "doubtful whether the participation of smaller states can really add very much to the ability of the great powers to assure stability of international life."[41] Those critics who suppose that Kennan's wish for a more broadly based power balance derives somehow from fuzzy sentiment—critics such as Lord Chalfont, in the headnote to this chapter, who appears not to know any better; and Dean Acheson, who does know better, in his now-famous comment that "Kennan has never . . . grasped the realities of power relationships"—are mistaken.[42]

---

[40]"'X' Plus 25: Interview with George F. Kennan," p. 14.

[41]Kennan, *American Diplomacy*, p. 86.

[42]Lord Chalfont, "Why America Must Ignore This Man," *The Times*, May 2, 1978; Acheson, quoted in *U.S. News & World Report*, January 17, 1958.

When Kennan speaks of world equilibrium, it must be remembered, he is thinking almost exclusively of Europe and the industrial Far East. There is something of a Northern hemispheric bias in this, as Kennan himself concedes, but the position is more properly traced back to Kennan's concept of five global power centers. If those five centers are kept in balance, he believes, the international system will find equilibrium without too much regard for the rest of the globe. If they are not, nothing done in the rest of the globe stands a chance of achieving a balance.

What Kennan objects to is the notion that "balance" requires superpower hegemony or a crude division of the world into Soviet and American spheres. True, he recalls in his *Memoirs*, America's strength and Europe's exhaustion at the close of World War II had created a temporary arrangement of Soviet–American dominance (a "great geopolitical disbalance"), but he never thought such dominance could or should last. Kennan wanted

> to get us as soon as possible out of the position of abnormal political–military responsibility in Western Europe which the war had forced upon us. I had no confidence that a *status quo* dependent on so wide an American commitment could be an enduring one. Such bipolarity, I thought, might do for a few years; it could not endure indefinitely. . . . [We could not hold] Western Europe indefinitely in some sort of paternal tutelage. Some day, it appeared to me, this divided Europe, dominated by the military presences of ourselves and the Russians, would have to yield to something more natural—something that did more justice to the true strength and interests of the intermediate European peoples themselves.[43]

This position was reflected consistently in Kennan's writings in the immediate postwar period, when he rarely lost an

---

[43]Kennan, *Memoirs* I, pp. 463, 464.

opportunity to call for measures that would restore independence and strength to the Continent.

Three factors persuaded Kennan against any idea of immediate disengagement from Europe as the war drew to a close: Europe's weakness and dislocation; the Soviet army's domination of Eastern Europe and parts of the Far East, leaving it without serious rival on the Continent; and the general fluidity of the power balance in the first few years after the war. No new order had yet congealed. The defeat—dismemberment, really—of Germany had left a great power vacuum, and there seemed to be some danger that the Soviets could come to achieve what Kennan believed America must prevent above all: the control of more than one great center of military–industrial power. American security always had and always would require that "no single Continental land power should come to dominate the entire Eurasian land mass."[44]

The military realities of the war's end, not the Yalta agreement or any other paper treaty, dictated that the Soviet Union would dominate Eastern Europe. For this Kennan blamed the allied demand for Germany's unconditional surrender ("only another way of saying that the war had to be fought until the Allied and Russian armies met *somewhere*") in combination with the Western refusal to create a second front in Europe well before 1944. That is, the allies had both consigned the postwar future of Eastern Europe to the military outcome there and failed to play an important role in that outcome.[45] The *somewhere* where Russian and Western troops met was the Elbe River, across which the two sides have glared and bristled ever since.

I cannot fail to say a word here about containment as a strategic doctrine, though its methods and tactics will be discussed in another chapter. It should by now be abun-

---

[44]NWC lecture, "Contemporary Problems of Foreign Policy," September 17, 1948, *Kennan Papers*, Box 17; Kennan, *American Diplomacy*, p. 10.

[45]Kennan, *Russia and the West*, p. 362.

dantly clear that Kennan distinguished sharply among geographical areas, and that he sought to strengthen the allies in order to recreate something approximating the nineteenth-century Concert of Europe. On the other hand, this last goal could not be accomplished in one fell swoop. The United States would have to take primary responsibility, at least for the time being, for countering the Soviets.

Kennan never believed that Soviet leaders, at the close of the war or at any time since, would be willing to take serious risks of another all-out war to achieve their limited political ends.[46] Even the X-Article, which looks alarmist by some standards today, emphasized: "the Russians . . . should not be considered as embarked on a do-or-die program to overthrow our society by a given date. The theory of the inevitability of the eventual fall of capitalism has the fortunate connotation that there is no hurry about it."[47] But there was always the chance of a military threat, as well as of even more dangerous (at the time) political and psychological threats to the self-confidence of Europe. Gaddis writes that the overall plan of containment was as follows:

> By the end of 1948, Kennan had come to regard three steps as necessary to accomplish [a favorable equilibrium]: (1) restoration of the balance of power through the encouragement of self-confidence in nations threatened by Soviet expansionism; (2) reduction, by exploiting tension between Moscow and the international communist movement, of the Soviet Union's ability to project influence beyond its borders; (3) modification, over time, of the Soviet concept of

---

[46]He stressed this point repeatedly. See "Current Problems of Soviet–American Relations," lecture delivered at Naval Academy, Annapolis, on May 9, 1947, *Kennan Papers*, Box 17; NWC lecture, "Where Are We Today?" December 21, 1948, *Kennan Papers*, Box 17; unsent letter to Walter Lippmann, April 6, 1948, quoted in *Memoirs* I, p. 361; and *The Cloud of Danger*, pp. 151–200.

[47][Kennan], "The Sources of Soviet Conduct," pp. 572–73.

international relations, with a view to bringing about a
negotiated settlement of outstanding differences.

Containment, in other words, would not have to last
forever.[48]

Once it became clear that Europe was stable, Kennan
believed, the Soviets might—just might—be willing to
withdraw their forces from the region, provided America
and Britain did likewise. This outcome was highly to be
desired, for until it happened there could be no independent
Europe and no improved world order. But what would
happen to Germany in the event of such a withdrawal? The
German question had helped spark two world wars. Now it
became central to Kennan's postwar thinking as well.

Kennan kept coming back to Germany and disengagement throughout the early 1950s, in the first years of his
second career as historian and publicist. European recovery,
both economic and spiritual, was now well in hand. The cold
war was at its height. By 1957, the Soviets had launched
Sputnik, tested their first intercontinental ballistic missile,
and crushed the Hungarian uprising. Stalin was four years
dead. Much had changed since the close of the war. Now
Kennan touched off possibly the greatest public explosion of
his career.

In the Reith Lectures of 1957, delivered over BBC radio
and heard by millions in Europe and later around the world,
Kennan suggested that the division of Europe was no longer
tolerable. There were those in Europe, he acknowledged,
who believed a divided Germany "to be less of a problem to
them than was the united Germany of recent memory." This
view could easily be understood, and it had once been
justified.

---

[48]Gaddis, *Strategies of Containment*, pp. 36–37. Thus does Kennan now
write, in *Memoirs* I, p. 367, that Stalin's death, the end of international
Communist solidarity, and the now-accomplished "mellowing" of Soviet
power "not only invalidated the original concept of containment, [but]
disposed in large measure of the very concept which it addressed."

But there is danger in permitting it to harden into a permanent attitude. It expects too much, and for too long a time, of the United States. . . . It does less than justice to the strength and the abilities of the Europeans themselves. It leaves unsolved the extremely precarious and unsound arrangements which now govern the status of Berlin. . . . It takes no account of the present dangerous situation in the satellite area. It renders permanent what was meant to be temporary. It assigns half of Europe, by implication, to the Russians.[49]

Where once Kennan had toyed with a plan to partition Germany back into "the small kingdoms, the chocolate soldiers, the picturesque localisms" of the eighteenth century,[50] he now believed it should be unified and—though he never used the word at the time—neutralized.

As usual, Kennan avoided precise and premised arguments in favor of what Acheson would call, with evident exasperation, "musings, wonderings, questionings, suggestions."[51] But the meaning of his central passage was fairly clear:

Might it not just be that the only politically feasible road to unification and independence for Germany should lie precisely through her acceptance of certain restraints on freedom to shape her future military position in Europe? And, if so, is it not just a bit quixotic to cling, in the name of German freedom and independence, to a position which implies the sacrifice of all freedom and all independence for many millions of Germans, namely the people of Eastern Germany, for an indefinite time to come? No useful purpose is going to be served by the quest for perfect solutions.[52]

---

[49]Later published as *Russia, the Atom and the West*, pp. 39–40.

[50]Memorandum to Sumner Welles, February 1940, quoted in *Memoirs* I, p. 119.

[51]Dean Acheson, "The Illusion of Disengagement," *Foreign Affairs*, April 1958, p. 374.

[52]Kennan, *Russia, the Atom and the West*, pp. 43–44.

By "certain restraints on freedom to shape her military position" Kennan had in mind, certainly, that a united Germany could not join either of the military alliances that marked the division of Europe. He seemed also to be thinking of more radically extending the zone of neutrality. Of his position at the close of the war he would later write: "I . . . wanted to hold the door open to permit the eventual emergence of large areas (a united, demilitarized Germany, a united Europe, a demilitarized Japan) that would be in the military sense uncommitted, as between the two worlds."[53]

Acheson, who had always thought Kennan's ideas on disengagement a bit "mystical,"[54] wrote in *Foreign Affairs* that Kennan's neutralization plan was "quite fantastic":

> Whatever Germans might initially think they would be willing to do, there is no precedent in history for, nor does there seem to me to be any possibility of, the successful insulation of a large and vital country situated, as Germany is, between two power systems and with ambitions and purposes of its own. . . . [I]t would not be long, I fear, before there would be an accommodation of some sort or another between an abandoned Germany and the great Power to the East. Under this accommodation, a sort of new Ribbentrop–Molotov agreement, the rest of the free world would be faced with what has twice been so intolerable as to provoke world war—the unification of the European land mass (this time the Eurasian land mass) under a Power hostile to national independence and individual freedom.[55]

It may be noted that Acheson was using Kennan's own favorite argument (about the military–industrial potential of the Eurasian land mass) against him; Kennan could hardly take issue with that. The root difference between Kennan

---

[53]Kennan, *Memoirs* I, p. 463.
[54]Quoted in *U.S. News & World Report*, January 17, 1958.
[55]Acheson, "The Illusion of Disengagement," p. 378.

and Acheson, to which I shall return presently, was on the workings of a balance of power in application: to wit, what would an independent Germany do if pressured by one of the two preeminent world powers?

In any case, Acheson need hardly have worried about what the Germans "might initially think they would be willing to do." Konrad Adenauer, West Germany's chancellor, vigorously denied that neutrality was the path to unification. Kennan was denounced from all sides on the floor of the *Bundestag*. The closest thing to a public defense of his views in Germany came from his friend Carlo Schmidt: "Why, after all, should so prominent [*bedeutender*] a man not have for once a scurrilous thought?"[56]

In retrospect, it is hard to see how the Germans could have reacted otherwise, and not only for reasons relating to the cold war. For a self-described realist, Kennan offered very slender evidence to support the wishful notion that *Germany*, of all the European powers—the Germany of Bismarck, Kaiser Wilhelm, and Hitler; the Germany that comprised one of five great concentrations of military–industrial power in the world—could long be kept neutral, still less demilitarized, by some sort of treaty agreement. Disengagement might be a good idea, but if its corollary was a meek and disarmed Germany, it seemed an unlikely prospect. To hold that all the potential power of a united Germany could be kept shackled forever flew in the face of everything Kennan believed about power realities and artificial structures.

The balance-of-power argument between Kennan and Acheson is a good deal harder to reckon. That argument would recur through the rest of Kennan's career, most recently in reference to *The Cloud of Danger*. Kennan, it will be recalled, tried in this book to delimit American security interests around the world. Clearly recognizing the difficulty created for any such plan by the precedent of Korea, he

---

[56]Quoted in Kennan, *Memoirs* II, pp. 249–52.

wrote the following about South Korea in 1977: "Today, circumstances are quite different. There is a fully independent and stable Japanese government. . . . Power in Moscow is in the hands of people who . . . represent a great change from the Soviet regime of Stalin's last years."[57] To this Edward N. Luttwak replied:

> Unfortunately one cannot order à la carte; the Japanese undoubtedly much prefer alliance with the United States, but they can hardly continue indefinitely to consign their security to our hands if we persevere in dismantling the military strength which is their protection. If forced to do so, they will reach a more secure accommodation with others. . . . If Mr. Kennan wants to order Japan, he must follow the set menu and have South Korea also.[58]

The parallel between Luttwak's and Acheson's argument is striking. They both contend that a nation of considerable power (Japan or Germany, respectively), when faced with pressure from a greater power (the Soviet Union), would seek "accommodation" with that power. Kennan, though as always he says little of it explicitly, evidently believes just the reverse: that the smaller power has means of resisting pressure; that where those means fail, the smaller power will seek closer association with another power (the United States) *against* the threatening power; and that in real life the likelihood of pressure from the Soviet Union is slight.

I hesitate to take sides in this dispute, seeing as—to be Kennan-like—it would seem to be largely an empirical matter and likely to vary with the circumstances. Perhaps both Kennan and his critics are a bit too rigid. Kennan, certainly, seems too willing to assume a political will to resist in the threatened power. This is especially evident in his

---

[57] Kennan, *The Cloud of Danger*, p. 112.

[58] Luttwak, "The Strange Case of George F. Kennan," reprinted in Martin F. Herz, ed., *Decline of the West? George Kennan and His Critics* (Washington: Ethics and Public Policy Center, 1978), pp. 102–3.

recent discussions of "Finlandization," the process by which, some conservatives allege, Europe risks losing its political freedom of action to Soviet political–military pressure. "In terms of population and industrial potential," Kennan told George Urban, "Western Europe is at least fully equal to the Soviets. . . . 'Finlandization', if it ever comes, will be a self-inflicted wound."[59]

IV

So much for great powers. What about American interests and strategy in the rest of the world?

Well, not much.

Always skeptical about the desirability and prospects of American intimacy with the developing nations, Kennan has become positively indifferent to most of the globe in his most recent writings. He is, as Ullman wrote in a review of *The Cloud of Danger*, "unequivocally for retrenchment."[60] And although Kennan's brand of "isolationism" is most often coolly sophisticated, it has an unfortunate tendency to descend now and then into the sort of peevish self-centeredness that gave midwestern isolationism a bad name.

To be sure, much of Kennan's indifference to the non-European world is a natural consequence of his lifelong preoccupations with power relationships and America's internal health. The Third World has precious little to do with either. "If [the] physical intactness of our [world] can be preserved," Kennan once wrote, "I am not too worried about our ability to find answers to the more traditional problems

---

[59]Kennan and Urban, "A Conversation," p. 20. See also pp. 58–59; and Kennan, *The Cloud of Danger*, pp. 144–46.

[60]Ullman, "The 'Realities' of George F. Kennan," p. 145. Kennan began calling for a "semi-isolationism" as early as 1968. See *Democracy and the Student Left*, p. 159.

of international life."[61] Kennan is not even *that* optimistic nowadays. It is hard to think clearly or long about relations with Zaire or even Panama when you believe the United States is on the verge of both nuclear war and irreparable internal decay.

Moreover, Kennan feels sure that, even if the non-European world were strategically important, it would be in no serious danger from the Soviet Union. In occupied Prague in the late 1930s, Kennan came to believe in

> the continued and undiminished relevance in the modern world of Gibbon's assertion that "there is nothing more contrary to nature than the attempt to hold in obedience distant provinces." Out of this grew my feeling that one must not be too frightened of those who aspire to world domination. No one people is great enough to establish a world hegemony.

"What I am asserting," Kennan said at Oxford in 1957, "is that universal world dominion is a technical impossibility." It was for precisely this reason that Kennan had objected to the implications of the Truman Doctrine: a universal commitment to defend nations threatened by "armed minorities" or "outside pressure." He thought it more prudent to ensure before intervention that (a) "the problem at hand is one within our economic, technical, and financial capabilities"; (b) without intervention the resulting situation "might redound very decidedly to the advantage of our political adversaries"; and (c) the favorable results of intervention would "carry far beyond the limits of the [nation assisted] itself." This, obviously, was a prescription for considerable restraint. And Kennan has little use for nonstrategic relationships.[62]

---

[61]Kennan, *Russia and the West*, p. 398; see also *American Diplomacy*, pp. 9, 12, 23; *Realities of American Foreign Policy*, p. 28; *Russia, the Atom and the West*, pp. 11–12.

[62]Kennan, *Memoirs* I, p. 129; *Russia and the West*, p. 276; NWC lecture, "Orientation and Comments on National Security Problem," *Kennan Papers*, Box 17. See also Kennan and Urban, "A Conversation," p. 23.

Whatever else their merits, Kennan's writings on relations with the international hoi polloi can be read as "a kind of manual for diplomats, a healthy corrective to the more usual"—grandiose—"approaches to international relations, to be read with profit by any American embarking on an assignment (or a career) representing this country in relationships with foreign officials."[63] Kennan's sense of limits, never dull, is especially acute here.

It cannot be discounted, finally, that Kennan has no experience with and little appreciation for non-Western cultures, other than that of Russia and perhaps Japan. His entire diplomatic career, as he forthrightly concedes, was spent in high northern latitudes: Lisbon, on the same latitudinal circle as Washington, D.C., was his southernmost post. "The negative impressions produced by occasional brief encounters with places farther south . . . were largely, I am sure, the result of . . . blind spots," Kennan wrote in 1967. "As such, they were no doubt shallow and misleading. But they, too, affected—for better or for worse—future thoughts and outlooks on international affairs."[64] Kennan's diaries in a 1944 trip through Iraq are typical of those quoted in his *Memoirs*. They refer, like some disgruntled tourist, to "selfishness and stupidity," a populace "unhygienic in its habits," and a tendency to "religious bigotry and fanaticism."[65]

With all this, it should hardly come as a surprise that Kennan casts a cold eye on interdependence and has virtually nothing in the way of a positive program for the Third World. He regrets, in some sense, its very existence— deploring the proliferation of sovereignty since the second world war for its tendency to separate power from responsibility and create ungovernable mini-nations. He even feels compelled to place the term "Third World" in quotation marks at times, as if to deny its legitimacy as an analytic

---

[63]Ullman, "The 'Realities' of George F. Kennan," p. 149.
[64]Kennan, *Memoirs* I, p. 181.
[65]Quoted in ibid., pp. 184–85.

category. He does not understand the all-fired rush to development, anyway, and he seems to believe—in an unfortunately well-publicized passage—that the Third World can develop as he thinks his native Wisconsin did, entirely by means of self-reliance, hard work, and thrift.[66]

I do not mean to belittle Kennan's global views. As always, he brings his novelist's eye for detail and a capacity for panoramic overview into the analysis, and he develops fine critiques of the conventional reliance on foreign aid and far-flung security pacts. But the critiques are entirely negative—the species of argument that tells all you want to know about what is *wrong* with something and very little about how to set it right. The preeminent theme in *The Cloud of Danger* is that Kennan does not like the postwar topography of international life, sees no early way back to a better system, and therefore wants to have as little to do with it as possible:

> I shall now attempt to describe, by way of summary, what [my global grand design] would look like. One would begin with a realistic recognition of the many limitations that rest upon the United States government. . . . [W]e would face the consequences of this relative helplessness. . . . This means, of course, the reduction of external commitments to the indispensable minimum. . . . This would involve the abandonment of several obsolescent and nonessential positions: notably those at Panama, in the Philippines, and in Korea. . . . In the case of Southern Africa we would take cognizance of the tragic profundity of the conflicts with which that region is racked. . . . As for the rest of the Third World, we would take account, again, of our general helplessness in the face of its problems. . . . With relation to China, we would tread warily and not too fast. . . .[67]

The list goes on. The message is the same.

---

[66]Kennan, *The Cloud of Danger*, pp. 29, 37, 38–39.
[67]Ibid., pp. 233–35.

V

Kennan had observed in the first of his Stafford Little Lectures in 1954 that "American political thought came to be affected, in the postwar era, by a sort of schizophrenia." Foreign policy operated on two separate planes of international reality—the one frightening and dangerous, obsessed with security and the "law of the jungle," the other comfortable, traditional, concerned with the usual modest tasks of diplomacy. Kennan set his aim to reintegrate the two planes, and by the end of the last lecture he did so with a structural elegance that was breathtaking even by comparison with his other writing. He argued for the "essential unity of all the problems of our national behavior":

> To my own mind, the upshot of these considerations is that it is in the inner development of our civilization—in what we are to ourselves and not what we are to others—that these two planes of international reality really come together. We will not find the unity of foreign policy for which we are concerned if we seek it only in the fashioning of relationships external to our national life. We will find it only in the recognition of the full solemnity of our obligation as Americans of the twentieth century: the obligation of each of us, as an individual, to his God and his faith; the obligation of all of us, as a political society, to our own national ideals and through those ideals to the wider human community of which we are in ever increasing measure a part.[68]

The contrast of this measured optimism with Kennan's deep and bitter pessimism of today is disturbing. What happened? By what unrelenting heartbreak did Kennan lose his hopes between 1954 and 1977? The passage cited above—unifying national and international affairs—provides a clue. His answer to a question at the National War College

---

[68]Kennan, *Realities of American Foreign Policy*, pp. 28–30, 119–20.

in 1946 provides another. Military force, one student officer observed, was an essentially negative phenomenon in human affairs. Did the United States have something more positive to offer the world? Kennan replied, "I would be happier . . . and I think we would be on sounder ground, if we had things that were constructive to offer to other people in fields besides military fields. . . . I am still trying to think it out. . . . I just don't know."[69] Three decades ago, as I will discuss in coming chapters, Kennan already had his doubts about America's capacity to solve its urgent internal problems. Now he doubts no longer: it cannot.

---

[69]Question and answer period, NWC lecture, "Measures Short of War (Diplomatic)," September 16, 1946, *Kennan Papers*, Box 16.

THREE

On Morality in World Affairs

> "What giants?" asked Sancho Panza.
> "Those you see over there," replied his master, "with their long arms; some of them have them well nigh two leagues in length."
> "Take care, sir," cried Sancho. "Those over there are not giants but windmills. . . . "
> "It is clear," replied Don Quixote, "that you are not experienced in adventures. . . . "
>
> *Cervantes*

There is an uncreative tendency among commentators on foreign affairs to stamp quixotic whatever they believe to be impractical or unrealistic. Writers so stamped often retort, like Quixote, that they see reality more clearly, or more rightly, than their critics. (On this issue, Cervantes himself is ambivalent, notwithstanding the popular image of Quixote as madman or fool.) What is relevant about such controversies for this book is that George Kennan finds himself—the temptation is to say, as usual—on both sides. Most often he is Sancho Panza, warning with great agitation against some prevailing chimera.[1] But every now and then he switches roles, usually in questions involving nuclear war, and then it is he who risks becoming, in the eyes of one or another critic, like the gentleman from La Mancha.[2]

Behind this confusion of roles is a false dichotomy between facts and values, between reality and morality, as if it were necessary to choose one or the other. It is a dichotomy to which Kennan sometimes seems to subscribe, usually taking the side of "reality," although at other times his writing is rather openly value-laden. Kennan tends to reject the *general* case for morality as a criterion "for the determination of the behavior of states" and "for measuring and comparing the behavior of different states"[3]—but in *specific* instances he applies what are unquestionably moral standards to debates on precisely those subjects.

Even in his general argument on the question of morality in world affairs, Kennan is what philosophers call incoherent. If Kennan were writing philosophy, that would be a serious charge. And in fact there will occasionally appear in academic journals an article aiming to instruct Kennan, as if he were a slightly dull and opinionated undergraduate, on elementary political theory. A Columbia

---

[1] In his Reith Lectures, for example, as quoted in Chapter 2, Kennan asked, "[I]s it not just a bit quixotic to cling, in the name of German freedom and independence, to a position which implies the sacrifice of all freedom and all independence for many millions of Germans . . . ?" In *The Cloud of Danger*, he wrote that "whoever made it his objective to realize the dream of a democratically governed world in any short space of time . . . would be behaving very quixotically indeed" (p. 42). In *Democracy and the Student Left*, he wrote of the radical college student: "Romantic and quixotic, he is on the prowl for causes. His nostrils fairly quiver for the scent of some injustice he can sally forth to remedy" (p. 215).

[2] Tom Wicker began one column as follows: "No doubt George F. Kennan will be widely considered Quixotic for calling attention at this time to the 'collision course' on which he believes the nuclear superpowers are embarked . . ." (*The New York Times*, May 26, 1981).

[3] Kennan, *Realities of American Foreign Policy*, p. 49.

University professor, for instance, once complained about Kennan's "disjunctive quality" and went on ponderously to discover that "the truth lies somewhere between the Scylla of 'utopian' morality and the Charybdis of 'actual' reality."[4] That is all very well, and it is true, I believe, that critics like the Columbia professor have a (clichéd) point. But they also miss a point: Kennan is fully capable of grasping a philosophical argument—more capable, one suspects, than a great many of his critics—and if he does not choose to make one there is likely to be a reason. Anyone who cares to criticize Kennan's treatment of morality in foreign policy, as I will do some pages hence, must first try to get a grip on exactly what Kennan is saying and why.

It is a great injustice to read Kennan principally as a failed philosopher. He is not writing moral tracts, but histories and pragmatic guides to foreign policy. If there are blind spots or gaps in his moral reasoning, they could be called secondary and not primary flaws. Kennan may be faulted for a certain inconsistency, but only once the critic acknowledges Kennan's implicit defense of inconsistency. I will try to do one, then the other, in the pages that follow.

I

The first thing to understand about Kennan's view of the moral purposes of power is that he is not necessarily trying to make the argument that Charles Beitz calls "international skepticism"—an argument Beitz attributes, by implication, to Kennan.[5] International skepticism, which is associated

---

[4] Jonathan Knight, "George Frost Kennan and the Study of American Foreign Policy: Some Critical Comments," *Western Political Quarterly*, March 1967, p. 157.

[5] Charles R. Beitz, *Political Theory and International Relations* (Princeton: Princeton University Press, 1979), p. 13. He attributes "international skepticism" to Kennan by inference on pp. 12, 17n.

with the realist tradition, holds that morality has no place, or a very limited place, in discussions of foreign policy. But this is in itself a philosophical position. Kennan's is usually not: when he discusses morality (or "legal-moralism") explicitly, it is almost always to point out its confusing or illusory impact on a particular past or present diplomatic episode. And although there are times when Kennan seems to be making a general case against morality as a standard in international affairs, there are also times when he argues for upholding values and ideals.

To Kennan's way of thinking, power always creates a "moral dilemma":

> [T]o wield power is always at best an ambivalent thing—a sharing in the guilt taken upon themselves by all those men who, over the course of the ages, have sought or consented to tell others what to do. . . . Power, like sex, may be concealed or outwardly ignored, and in our society it often is; but neither in the one case nor in the other does this concealment save us from the destruction of our innocence or from the confrontation with the dilemmas these necessities imply.[6]

He does not, unfortunately, elaborate this passage. But his meaning is not far to seek. For beginning in his year at the National War College and continuing through most of his later career, Kennan has expended a quantity of agonized thought on the distinction between what the United States *would like* to do in world affairs and what it *can* do, or, if you like, between the ideal and the real.

Notwithstanding his deserved reputation as an anti-Utopian, Kennan does respect at least the motivations behind the idealistic strains in American political thought.

---

[6]Kennan, *Russia and the West*, pp. 397–98.

Those strains, he told a War College audience, are primarily products of the twentieth century, by which time the United States had conquered its own frontiers and assured itself ("as it seemed, at least") of its own prosperity. Americans then turned their gaze to the outside world, with

> a great deal of genuine goodwill and generosity of a purely American variety. This was a sort of Rotarian idealism and 'do-good-iness'. . . . I am not speaking in a deprecating sense of these phases of American thought and policy. They embrace something which is immensely vital and important and worthy . . . —a contribution of which every one of us can be proud.[7]

Just as he can admire idealism, Kennan is often disdainful of politics shorn from value. Referring to the glib public assertions of common purpose between Nazi Germany and the Soviet Union on the occasion of the 1939 Nonaggression Pact, Kennan writes: "You had the *reductio ad absurdum* of political cynicism, the demonstration of the helplessness of people who have cut loose from every subjective obligation of decency, and have launched themselves into a stratosphere of unlimited opportunism where there is no moral gravity."[8] Even Communist revolutionaries, with whom Kennan could hardly disagree more, get some credit for their sincerity: "I have had more respect for them, in all their error and in all their hopelessness, than for many pillars of respectable American society, vegetating in the smugness and selfishness and superficiality of their particular brand of philistinism."[9]

These are, it must be acknowledged, relatively rare expressions of sympathy for idealism. Much more often,

---

[7]NWC lecture, "What Is Policy?" December 18, 1947, *Kennan Papers*, Box 17.

[8]Kennan, *Russia and the West*, p. 335.

[9]Kennan, "The Ethics of Anti-Communism," p. 4.

Kennan writes of problems, limits, and illusions associated with idealism and moralism in foreign affairs. There are several themes in these writings, and they are very difficult to reconstruct—or construct—systematically.

First, "do-good-iness"—in its pure form, at least—stands on a premise about the world "which has been challenged by the realities of today." It requires, Kennan said in 1947, a world without power struggles, without all the harsh realities that were discussed in Chapter 2.[10]

Second, once America's idealists are moved to take account of the unhappy need for a balance of power, they will begin to find that there are two "patterns," one superimposed on the other, in considerations of foreign policy: "The underlying pattern [principles and ideals] is the forward-looking and—we hope—the permanent one. It is the one which is congenial to our instincts and our national spirit. The superimposed one [power realities] is something that has been forced on us by circumstances. . . . Our attention must perforce be concentrated on this second aspect of policy, for our national security stands or falls with it."[11]

Third, though the two patterns are in tension, they do not have to be seen as conflicting at root. Americans, Kennan said in effect, should recognize that their security is a precondition for a policy based on ideal principles:

> I think that our country has made the greatest effort in modern times to . . . induce people to treat the questions of international life from the standpoint of principles and not power; but even we in the end are compelled to consider the security of our people . . . because . . . unless they can enjoy that security they will never be able to make any useful contribution to a better and more peaceful world.

---

[10]NWC lecture, "What Is Policy?" *Kennan Papers*, Box 17.
[11]Ibid.

Ideals cannot survive anarchy or the dominance of international life by powers that have no respect for principle.[12]

Kennan says something like the same thing in a
statement that, in a roundabout way, argues that power
realities *transcend* any proper application of moral standards:
"[W]e find no greater readiness, so far, to admit the validity
and legitimacy of power realities and aspirations, to accept
them without feeling the obligation of moral judgment, to
take them as existing and inalterable human forces, neither
good nor bad, and to seek their point of maximum
equilibrium rather than their reform or their repression."[13]

To this point, power and morality have been portrayed
as essentially complementary concepts. Power realities,
Kennan has said, are both beyond morality themselves and a
necessary condition for the achievement of moral ends. But a
fourth theme, running through much of Kennan's other
work, opposes "security" and "principle" as deeply conflicting values. In writing of the movement toward war in the
1930s, he said:

> The Western democracies had contrived to get them-
> selves confronted, at one and the same time, with two
> powerful adversaries—one centered in Berlin, the other
> in Moscow. . . . The West had allowed itself to become
> so weak that it was not strong enough to defeat either
> one of these adversaries without the help of the other. It
> is important to remember this. It meant that as early as
> the late 1930s, no clean, moral victory for the West was
> any longer in the cards—no victory in the name of
> principle and ideals. *Only the very strong, or those so weak*
> *that they do not choose to compete in terms of power, can enjoy*
> *the luxury of acting purely in the name of ideals; the others*
> *have to make their compromises.*[14]

---

[12]"Current Problems of Soviet–American Relations," address prepared
for delivery at the Naval Academy, Annapolis, May 9, 1947, *Kennan Papers*,
Box 17.

[13]Kennan, *American Diplomacy*, p. 49.

[14]Kennan, *Russia and the West*, pp. 314–15 [emphasis added]. He
repeatedly refers to moral action as a "luxury." See also pp. 395–96;
Kennan, *American Diplomacy*, pp. 66–67, 68, 72–73.

This position sometimes found even sharper expression. "Only the very strong," he wrote in his diary of July 28, 1950, "can take high and mighty moral positions and ignore the possibilities of balance among the opposing forces. The weak must accept realities and exploit those realities to their advantage as best they can."[15]

A corollary to this fourth theme holds flatly that morality must be secondary to the national interest in foreign policy. "I cannot resist the thought," Kennan wrote in *American Diplomacy*, "that if we were able to

> refrain from constant attempts at moral appraisal—if, in other words, instead of making ourselves slaves of the concepts of international law and morality, we would confine these concepts to the unobtrusive, almost feminine, function of the gentle civilizer of national self-interest in which they find their true value— . . . then, I think, posterity might look back upon our efforts with fewer and less troubled questions."[16]

Later in the same volume, Kennan took the assertion a long step further—and, paradoxically, back to the third theme of the complementariness of national security and moral purposes—by appearing to state that the national interest and moral purposes are necessarily one and the same. Finishing an attack on rigid "legal-moralism," he pointed the way to a more sensible foreign policy:

> It will mean that we will have the modesty to admit that our own national interest is all that we are really capable of knowing and understanding—and the courage to recognize that if our purposes and undertakings here at home are decent ones, unsullied by arrogance or hostility toward other people or delusions of superiority, *then the pursuit of our national interest can never fail to be conducive to a better world.*[17]

---

[15]Quoted in *Memoirs* I, p. 495.
[16]Kennan, *American Diplomacy*, p. 50.
[17]Ibid., p. 88 [emphasis added].

This passage, it scarcely need be pointed out, begs crucial questions. Does Kennan think, for instance, that the national interest cannot fail to serve moral purposes, or that moral purposes cannot fail to serve the national interest? His comments elsewhere provide little clue. In one book he writes that "our purposes as a nation [are] on balance worthy ones, which can be pursued and achieved without injury to any other people. . . ."[18] In another he writes: "I never doubted, in those years [of government service], the basic decency of our national purpose."[19]

A fifth theme relating reality and morality is essentially agnostic: international life is too complex to admit of clean moral judgments. Kennan sounds this theme occasionally in his history. After describing the food blockade that was kept up around Germany for more than a year after the close of hostilities in World War II, and even after pointing out that this caused suffering primarily among "the poorest and most helpless elements of the civilian population," Kennan concludes with a demonstration of his normative restraint: "I do not mean to argue about whether the Germans 'deserved' this. I find this word 'deserve,' when applied to an entire people, too vague to have historical usefulness."[20] He makes this case also in general terms:

> Let us face it: in most international differences elements of right or wrong, comparable to those that prevail in personal relationships, are—if they exist at all, which is a question—simply not discernible to the outsider. Where is the right or wrong of the Kashmir dispute? I am glad that it is not my task to seek it. And how about the conflict between the Israeli[s] and the Arabs? The very establishment of the State of Israel, at which we

---

[18]Kennan, *Realities of American Foreign Policy*, p. 62.

[19]Kennan, *Memoirs* II, p. 322.

[20]Kennan, *Russia and the West*, p. 163. He might just as well have argued that, since "deserve" cannot apply to a whole people, the Germans did *not* deserve such treatment—or, in other words, that it was morally suspect.

Americans warmly connived, was—whether right or wrong—essentially an act of violence.[21]

A sixth theme might be called that of moral relativity. Even if international politics were not so complicated, Kennan seems to argue, the standards to be applied would not be obvious, because there are few if any universally accepted moral beliefs. This could be either the empirical argument that different cultures emphasize different values, or the entirely analytical (and more skeptical) argument that there can be no true resolution among conflicting values. Kennan is not clear on how much relativity he is arguing for: "[L]et us not assume that our moral values, based as they are on the specifics of our national tradition and the various religious outlooks represented in our country, necessarily have validity for people everywhere." Directly there follows a curious non sequitur: "In particular, let us not assume that the *purposes* of states, as distinct from the methods, are fit subjects for measurement in moral terms."[22]

Anyone who believes he can draw together these six disparate, often vague, sometimes contradictory themes into a coherent system of morality in world affairs—or in the purposes of American power—is welcome to try. It is certainly beyond my subtlety of understanding. What seems clear to me is that Kennan cannot sum himself up any better than I can. Only once does he make the attempt.

> Morality, then, as the channel to individual self-fulfillment—yes. Morality as the foundation of civic virtue, and accordingly as a condition precedent to successful democracy—yes. Morality in governmental method, as a matter of conscience and preference on the part of our people—yes. But morality as a general criterion for the determination of the behavior of states and above all as a criterion for measuring and compar-

---

[21]Kennan, *Realities of American Foreign Policy*, pp. 36–37.
[22]Ibid., p. 47 [emphasis in original].

ing the behavior of different states—no. Here other criteria, sadder, more limited, more practical, must be allowed to prevail.[23]

This passage, of course, does not bring together all Kennan's general arguments about morality in world affairs. (Nor could it, since some of them conflict.) Even if it did, it is—as they are—unable to withstand analysis, as I hope to suggest below.

II

I said at the start of this chapter that it is unfair to view Kennan principally as a failed philosopher of morality in foreign affairs. It cannot be overlooked, on the other hand, that he is partly that. Probably on no other subject are his views so confusing. Certainly on no other subject does his disdain for easy answers translate so consistently into a failure even to ask the hard questions.

It is not my intent here to measure Kennan's views against some fixed system of morality in foreign policy. Even if I were inclined to do so, I have found no such system that is fully satisfying, and it is beyond my competence to construct one. That aside, such an exercise would obscure Kennan's own views. For the next few pages, I will simply hold a few of those views up to closer scrutiny. Where Kennan fails to ask hard questions, I will try to ask them myself.

The discussion might best begin with the national interest. It will be recalled from Chapter 2 that Kennan believes in an irreducible national interest, and that, roughly stated, is to protect national security and promote the welfare of Americans. Both these goals, Kennan believes, call for level-headed attention to power realities and a stable

---

[23]Ibid., p. 49.

world order. Moreover, these goals—the collective "national interest"—are held to exist objectively, detached from any judgment of values. Thus does Kennan speak of "knowing" or "understanding" the national interest[24] instead of seeking, judging, constructing, or debating it. Finally, he appears to believe that these broad purposes or interests lead logically to specific policy goals that are similarly beyond the scope of moral judgment. Thus does he deny that "the *purposes* of states . . . are fit subjects for measurement in moral terms."[25]

This notion of a national interest is vulnerable on two grounds, and here—so basic are my observations—I fear I will begin to sound like that Columbia professor.

First, even Kennan's broadest premises on the national interest, however agreeable to however many commentators, are not objective. They assert values: national security and the welfare of Americans. These values are not plucked from the ether, nor can they be deduced from any objective statement of facts. It is axiomatic nowadays that there are descriptive statements and there are normative statements, and no quantity of logic can generate one from the other. The values—again, however defensible—must be chosen as a matter of preference and therefore may be challenged as such. Even so basic an assertion as that America should follow its *national* interest begs the question of whether and when it should subordinate that interest to some broader moral value.

Second, even if there were an objective national interest, and even if it were just what Kennan says it is, the policy goals that derived from it could not themselves be objective. If I were a policy planner and I kept careful notes on everything Kennan has ever written about the national interest and power realities, if I distilled from those notes a list of principles, and if I kept that list on my desk and

---

[24]See again *American Diplomacy*, p. 88.
[25]Ibid., p. 47.

consulted it every day—still, I could find in it no objective guide to specific action. The principles, however objective, could tell me very little about how to allocate scarce resources among conflicting and desirable goals. For that I would need values.

To put it another way: The ship's captain of Chapter 2, even were he to take as a given that he should steer clear of rocks and stormy weather, would still have plenty of room for choice as to course and speed. There must, after all, be more than one safe direction to sail in the whole wide ocean. Once the hazards are bypassed, the captain can indulge his preferences as to destination; he can proceed directly or by the scenic route; and if he sees another ship foundering, he can move ahead or stop to render aid. None of these choices can be made "objectively," so there is no reason why moral concerns should not enter into them. And once moral concerns do enter the choice, there is no obvious reason why the captain should be empowered to rule them out of order on any decision he makes. In short, there is nothing to suggest that the *purposes* of nations should, as Kennan maintains, be exempt from moral challenge.

In light of all this, it is hard to see as anything but confused Kennan's seeming assertion that morality must always be subordinate to the national interest. Not only does "national interest" comprehend values in itself, and not only is it so vague as to preclude its use as a guide to specific action, but the renunciation of self-interest under some circumstances is in any case one of the defining characteristics of moral action. Perhaps Kennan tried to account for this when he said that "if our purposes . . . here at home are decent ones . . . then the pursuit of our national interest can never fail to be conducive to a better world."[26] This sentence could be interpreted as meaning that certain moral purposes are intrinsic in the national interest, or, in other words, that morality *does* count in determining the national interest. But

---

[26]Ibid., p. 88.

this interpretation, besides conflicting with much that Kennan says less ambiguously elsewhere, would open national behavior to moral criticism, which Kennan presumably wishes to avoid.

One trouble with the sort of analysis I am doing here is that it fills space in unequal proportion to that of the original statements analyzed. I need not, I hope, scrutinize Kennan's every moral view in order to make my point. There are two more, however, that deserve special mention, and they are those which I listed as fifth and sixth in the first part of this chapter.

One of these I called agnostic: it holds that international disputes are so complicated, so deeply rooted in historical ambiguities and uncontrollable forces, as to render futile the attempt at moral judgment. "Where," Kennan asks, "is the right or wrong of the Kashmir dispute? . . . And how about the conflict between the Israeli[s] and the Arabs?"[27] If Kennan means nothing more than to warn against simplistic moralizing, or to maintain that some disputes are morally ambiguous, then he is hard to disagree with. It seems abundantly clear, however, that Kennan demands greater service from the point. He means it, apparently, as something close to a complete exclusion of moral judgments from international conflicts. If so, he fails to prove the unlikely case that all such conflicts are as morally ambiguous as the two he cites. Few would have great difficulty discovering elements of right and wrong in the repeated attempts by the United States to overthrow or kill Fidel Castro, for example.[28] Even Kennan's own examples work partly against him. There is, after all, not one unitary conflict "between the Israeli[s] and the Arabs." There are many such conflicts, and some of them—the one centering around the West Bank of the Jordan River, say—may be fitter subjects than others for moral judgment.

---

[27]Kennan, *Realities of American Foreign Policy*, pp. 36–37. In his *Memoirs* II, p. 288, Kennan adds, "[E]vil is complex rather than unitary."
[28]See Ullman, "The 'Realities' of George F. Kennan," p. 154.

Here Kennan might retort with the last of the points I wish to discuss. I used his example against him; now he might try to return the favor. Moral standards are relative, he would say, and the very fact that thinking people can reach antithetical positions on an issue such as the West Bank should suggest the difficulty of moral reasoning in international affairs. Fair enough: but so what? Even within a single culture, there can be considerable disagreement about moral standards. That fact should urge a certain degree of tolerance and circumspection in the passing of judgments, but it certainly cannot abolish right and wrong altogether. No society truly operates at the least common denominator of moral belief; nor do individuals reserve moral judgment for those species of right and wrong that any person would label so. If I have listened with an open mind to all sides of a dispute and then reasoned it out according to my own sense of values, I will eventually feel justified in drawing a moral conclusion, even if others disagree. Kennan no doubt does just this in his personal life, notwithstanding the "agnostic" and "relativistic" hedges that always enter into such a moral equation.

In the final analysis, Kennan never gives a persuasive account of why nation-states should not be held accountable morally for the consequences of their actions. Of course, the moral accountability of collectives is a troublesome issue in philosophy. But some obligations are easier to agree upon than others. To the extent that the state is an agent of its citizens, it surely takes on an obligation not to do certain things; whether it is also obliged positively to do other things is open to question. It is less troublesome, that is, to assert that there are things a state *ought not*, morally, to do than to assert that there are things a state *ought*, morally, to do. If I believe, for instance, that it is wrong to kill noncombatants in wartime, then I have no great difficulty saying it is as wrong for a state as for an individual to do so. But if I believe that people have an obligation to help feed the starving, it is not quite as clear that the state, as an agent, takes on that obligation.

III

I have already taken a certain liberty in organizing Kennan's writings on morality and critiquing what I perceive to be their general thrust. I will now take a second liberty and say that I do not believe Kennan entirely means what he seems to say in his broadest comments on morality as a purpose of American foreign policy. It seems to me that the generality of some of his language does a disservice to his specific positions, making him seem more like Charles Beitz's "international skeptic" than he is in fact.

It is for this reason that I have mentioned how little Kennan can be understood as a failed philosopher. He does not write systematically because he does not want to, for his objections to morality as a criterion for global politics are not so much principled as prudential. Kennan's primary point is that it is all we can do to keep the world physically intact; that moral questions are, in any case—for a variety of reasons—difficult to resolve in international life; and that, consequently, we should concentrate on the former and not the latter. Moreover, as I shall discuss in Chapter 4, Kennan sees frightening gaps between concept and execution in foreign policy, and he is skeptical that moral purposes could be made to translate into moral effects.[29] "Please understand," he told George Urban, "that for purposes of argument I am given to overstating a case; and that is one of the reasons why you accuse me of contradiction. If one wants to see both sides of a coin, one has, momentarily at least, to bring out each side in exaggerated relief."[30] Kennan,

---

[29]The following doubtless applies to Kennan's international as well as domestic politics: "I have seen more harm done in this world by those who tried to storm the bastions of society in the name of utopian beliefs, who were determined to achieve the elimination of all evil . . . within their own time, than by all the humble efforts of those who have tried to create a little order and civility and affection within their own intimate entourage, even at the cost of tolerating a great deal of evil in the public domain" (*Democracy and the Student Left*, p. 9).

[30]Kennan and Urban, "A Conversation," p. 63.

it is well to recall, has usually spoken out on issues of foreign affairs when impelled by a conviction that there was some great public misunderstanding. Perhaps it helps to account for the general tone of his remarks to reflect that, in Kennan's mind, Americans more often err on the side of the quixotic than the cynical.

The reverse side of Kennan's moral coin—the side that gets *him* called quixotic—is his view of war, and particularly of weapons of mass destruction. Anyone who doubts there is a moral component to Kennan's writing need only read his accounts of human conflict and physical destruction.

This strain of moralism runs through even the earliest available samples of Kennan's writing, but especially those following World War II. In a public speech delivered soon after his recall from Moscow to help set up the War College, Kennan said the United States had two obligations for which it needed military power: first, to win any conflict it had to fight and, second, "to make sure that there should be no such conflict." This last was a "general and unwritten commitment" incumbent upon all "who wish to see the standards of decency and tolerance and international security upheld."[31]

This thought was extended when he returned to Hamburg in March, 1949, and saw the ruthlessly efficient handiwork of three days and nights of saturation bombing in 1943:

> Here, for the first time, I felt an unshakable conviction that no momentary military advantage . . . could have justified this stupendous, careless destruction of civilian life and of material values. . . . And it suddenly appeared to me that in these ruins there was an unanswerable symbolism which we in the West could not afford to ignore. If the Western world was really

---

[31]"Requirements of National Security," remarks to the National Defense Committee, Chamber of Commerce of the United States, January 23, 1947, *Kennan Papers*, Box 16.

going to make valid the pretense of a higher moral departure point . . . then it had to learn to fight its wars morally as well as militarily, or not fight them at all; for moral principles were a part of its strength. . . . The military would stamp this as naive; they would say that war is war, that when you're in it you fight with every means you have, or go down in defeat. But if that is the case, then there rests upon Western civilization, bitter as this may be, the obligation to be militarily stronger than its adversaries by a margin sufficient to enable it to dispense with those means which can stave off defeat only at the cost of undermining victory.[32]

Here there is no waffling, no suppressed morality, no disguised normative appeal. Kennan is asserting a value, openly and eloquently. It is a value that will follow him through discussions of tactical nuclear warfare, the carpet bombings of North Vietnam, and, finally, the strategic arms race.[33]

If anything has provoked Kennan's moral ire, it has been reliance on the nuclear warhead to prop up America's military posture. The atom bomb, Kennan said in his Einstein Award remarks of 1981, is "only something with which, in a moment of petulance or panic, you commit such fearful acts of destruction as no sane person would ever wish to have upon his conscience. . . . [W]e alone, so help us God, . . . have used the weapon in anger against others, and against tens of thousands of helpless noncombatants at that. I know that reasons were offered for [this]. I know that

---

[32]Diary entry, quoted in *Memoirs* I, p. 437.

[33]To follow this whole line of thinking would be a chapter in itself. See, for example: *Memoirs* I, pp. 261, 311, 471, 473; *Memoirs* II, pp. 59–60, 110, 247; *The Cloud of Danger*, p. 205; Kennan and Urban, "A Conversation," p. 65; "What Is Policy?" *Kennan Papers*, Box 17. Kennan has also rejected reciprocity as a justification for immoral violence: "And if the argument be that unreasoning cruelty on their [Vietcong's] part justifies the same on ours, then it must be asked: Since when have our standards of conduct been defined for us by our enemies?" ("What We've Lost in Vietnam," *The Washington Post*, January 14, 1973.)

others might have taken this sort of lead, had we not done so. But let us not, in the face of this record, so lose ourselves in self-righteousness and hypocrisy as to forget our own measure of complicity in creating the situation we face today."[34]

Nearly a year before the Einstein speech, in a less noticed address in West Germany, Kennan delivered perhaps the most impassioned lines of his life, directed at both Soviet and American leaders:

> For the love of God, for the love of your children and of the civilization to which you belong, cease this madness. You are mortal men. You are capable of error. You have no right to hold in your hands—there is no one wise enough and strong enough to hold in his hands—destructive powers sufficient to put an end to civilized life on a great portion of our planet. You have a duty not just to the generation of the present—you have a duty to civilization's past, which you threaten to render meaningless, and to its future, which you threaten to render nonexistent. No one should wish to have in his hands such powers. Thrust them from you. The risks you might thereby assume are not greater—could not be greater—than those which you are now incurring for us all.[35]

Kennan's passion, for all its eloquence, is carefully delimited. No matter how strongly he believes, for instance, that it is wrong to kill noncombatants, he has not—with only one exception—favored attempting to enforce this judgment among other nations.[36] And he has consistently maintained that, whatever the sympathies of the United States, it is none of its business how other governments treat their citizens.

---

[34]Address delivered on the occasion of receiving the Albert Einstein Peace Prize, May 19, 1981, at the Washington Marriott Hotel.

[35]Quoted in *The Washington Post*, May 24, 1981 [address delivered October, 1980].

[36]The one exception is that Kennan favored executing high Nazi leaders on sight at the close of World War II (*Memoirs* I, p. 260). He does not elaborate.

"No people," he wrote in 1951, "can be the judge of another's domestic institutions and requirements. . . ."[37] It was Kennan, in fact, who unearthed in historical researches the now widely cited quotation from John Quincy Adams: "[America] goes not abroad in search of monsters to destroy. She is the well-wisher of freedom and independence to all. She is the champion and vindicator only of her own."[38] In "Democracy as a World Cause," written in 1977, Kennan was even moved to place the words "dictatorship," "majority rule," and "democracy" in quotation marks, and he went on to maintain that any administration that set as its objective a democratically governed world "would be behaving very quixotically indeed."[39]

And so I am back where I started: with morality, reality, and Quixote. Kennan, I am free to confess, puzzles me no end in his discussions of morality in world affairs. Of course—obviously—the United States cannot make human rights or any other moral objective the sole guide to its foreign policy. But why can it not work toward these ends within the constraints of reality? Why *should* it not? John Quincy Adams, perhaps, might not have been so sanguine about America's liberties if he stopped to recall that they were won substantially on account of the intervention of France. And perhaps Kennan would stop disdaining the quixotic if he reminded himself that Quixote's ends were often as just as his means were bizarre:

> Here lies the noble fearless knight,
> Whose valor rose to such a height;
> When death at last did strike him down,
> His was the victory and renown.

---

[37]Kennan, *American Diplomacy*, p. 49.
[38]Address before the mid-winter dinner meeting of the Pennsylvania State Bar Association, January 16, 1953, manuscript, p. 5.
[39]Kennan, *The Cloud of Danger*, pp. 41–46.

He reck'd the world of little prize,
And was a bugbear in men's eyes;
But had the fortune in his age
To live a fool and die a sage.[40]

Such was Quixote's epitaph. Kennan, in renouncing nearly all talk of moral purpose for fear of limits and constraints, does not merely correct Quixote. He errs in the opposite direction.

---

[40]Walter Starkie, translator, *Don Quixote of La Mancha* (New York: New American Library, 1979), p. 1049.

III

THE PURVEYORS
OF POWER

FOUR

On Democratic Decisionmaking

> Sometimes I've been charged with being an elitist. Of *course* I am. What do people expect? God forbid that we should be without an elite. Is everything to be done by gray mediocrity?
>
> *Kennan*

On the Tuesday afternoon of October 1, 1946, George Kennan delivered a lecture at the Naval War College in Newport, Rhode Island, and there he said just about the most optimistic words he would ever manage on the subject of American democracy. "Now," he told his audience, "the real question is this: is a democracy capable of disposing of its strength in peacetime in such a way as to achieve [its foreign policy] ends? Can we possibly have the political flexibility and coordination which are necessary to this purpose? Well, if you ask me whether we have it now, my answer is no." To this, for the first and very nearly the last time in his recorded life, Kennan added a "but": "But if you ask me whether we *can* have such flexibility and such coordination of policy, I can only say that I don't see why not."[1]

Hardly exuberant, that. Still, there was at least a note of hope. Kennan was riding the tide of popularity of his "long telegram," and perhaps the apparent willingness to pay him heed helped persuade him that American foreign policy was on the verge of some new coherence and focus.[2] The feeling did not last. Just over a year later, with seven months as a high-level planner behind him,[3] Kennan first articulated— here in his private notes—the more pessimistic view of democracy that would stay with him, and intensify, for the next 35 years:

> When I returned from Russia, a year and a half ago . . . I was conscious of the weakness of the Russian position, of the slenderness of the means with which they operated, of the ease with which they could be pushed back. It was I who pressed for "containment," and for aid to Europe as a form of containment.
>
> Today, I think I was wrong—not in my analysis of the Soviet position, but in my assumption that this Government had the ability to "operate" politically at all, in the foreign field.[4]

Actually, Kennan's disenchantment with democratic decisionmaking was not quite so complete in 1947 as these

---

[1]Unpublished lecture, "Russia," Naval War College, Newport, Rhode Island, October 1, 1946, *Kennan Papers*, Box 16 [emphasis in original].

[2]Later, in his *Memoirs* II, pp. 320–21, Kennan suggested that the period from 1945 to 1949—the period of his own greatest influence—was virtually the only time in American history "when the conduct of America's peacetime diplomacy may be said to have had its own integrity. . . ." It is hard not to see elements of egocentricity in this.

[3]Kennan became head of George Marshall's Policy Planning Staff and began drafting what would become the Marshall Plan in late April of 1947.

[4]Private paper, "Notes on the Marshall Plan," December 15, 1947, *Kennan Papers*, Box 23. Like much of the contents of the Kennan Papers, this draft appears to have been written for Kennan's personal use only.

private notes make it seem. But his feeling was growing that the government needed major, structural change. His inability to persuade himself in later years that such a change was possible—or, in the end, entirely desirable—would leave him disillusioned, sometimes bitter, and inclined to believe that America is irremediably a shackled and clumsy participant in world affairs.

I

Even without the bother of Congress, public opinion, and a president with one eye always on domestic politics, the conduct of foreign affairs would be tricky enough. Kennan has always had the most earnest respect for the capacity of individuals—and, more potent still, of bureaucracies—to make hash of the clearest presidential directive and work horrors, with the best of intent, on the interests of the United States. Both his memoirs and his histories are full of what he calls the "farcical and near-tragic confusions" inflicted by crossed signals and incompetence on the conduct of foreign affairs.[5] Merely to read of Kennan's own experience in the diplomatic corps is to be convinced that international politics is a clumsy game indeed.[6] His histories, too, are full of boggling confusions.[7]

Even without all the tomfoolery—there is no other word for it—policy planning in Kennan's eyes is maddeningly

---

[5]Kennan, *Memoirs* I, p. 173.

[6]Anyone interested in such stories should turn particularly to Chapters 6 and 7 of Kennan's *Memoirs* I, where he tells with great wit and horror of the truly collossal ineptitude he has witnessed in official Washington.

[7]See, for example, *Memoirs* I, pp. 164–88; *The Decline of Bismarck's European Order,* esp. pp. 11–26, 250–65, 347–61; *Russia Leaves the War* (Princeton: Princeton University Press, 1956), esp. pp. 71–74, 191–218, 330–43, 397–412; *The Decision to Intervene* (Princeton: Princeton University Press, 1958), esp. pp. 31–57, 136–65, 405–29; *Russia and the West,* pp. 91–119.

hard. The heart of the task is "the shaping and conduct of policy for areas about which [planners] cannot be expert and learned,"[8] amidst tuggings of bureaucratic politics that would distort even the most expert decisions.[9] Two months after taking the job as George Marshall's Policy Planning Director, Kennan told a War College audience that "it seems like centuries" since he "could sit down here in my office . . . and divide the world into neat, geometric patterns." He could no longer enjoy leisurely abstraction. His job, he said, in one of his best extended metaphors, was like running his 235-acre farm:

> On every one of those acres, I have discovered, things are constantly happening. . . . The days . . . pass in a . . . succession of alarms and excursions. Here a bridge is collapsing. No sooner do you start to repair it than a neighbor comes to complain about a hedgerow which you haven't kept up—a half-mile away on the other side of the farm. At the very moment your daughter arrives to tell you that someone left the gate to the hog pasture open and the hogs are out. On the way to the hog pasture you discover that the beagle hound is happily liquidating one of the children's pet kittens. In burying the kitten you look up and notice that a whole section of the barn roof has been blown off, and needs instant repair. Somebody shouts pitifully from the bathroom window that the pump must have busted—there's no water in the house. At that moment a truck arrives with five tons of stone for the lane. And as you stand helplessly there, wondering which of these crises to attend to first, you notice the farmer's little boy standing silently before you with that maddening smile that is halfway a leer, and when you ask him what's up, he says triumphantly: "The bull's busted out and he's eating the strawberry bed."

---

[8]Kennan, *American Diplomacy*, pp. 37–38.
[9]See, for example, *Memoirs I*, pp. 372, 427–28, 465.

That's the only way I know to tell you what policy planning is like. The world is a big world. It has at least two hundred thirty-five big acres on it. . . . A nimble and astute person, working furiously against time, may indeed succeed in getting himself to a point where he thinks that with respect to one of those two hundred thirty-five acres he is some three or four months ahead of events. . . . But by the time he has gotten his ideas down on paper, the three or four months have mysteriously shrunk to that many weeks. By the time he has gotten those ideas accepted by others, they have become days. And by the time others have translated those ideas into action, it develops that the thing you were planning for took place day before yesterday, and everyone wants to know why in hell you did not foresee it a long time ago.[10]

Little wonder that Kennan frets when the farmers are squabbling, wandering off to promote pet projects, forming feuding coalitions, and pausing at frequent intervals to hold elections. It is hard to imagine any government, by Kennan's standards, that would be well constituted for the conduct of foreign affairs. But a democracy, with its penchant for bombast and gid, is in Kennan's view scarcely constituted at all.

II

Simply the quantity of Kennan's fulmination on democracy demands attention. It is safe to say that no theme takes up more space in Kennan's collected writings that that of the myopia, dilettantism, and inefficiency of democratic foreign

---

[10]NWC lecture, "Planning of Foreign Policy," June 18, 1947, *Kennan Papers*, Box 17. Kennan quotes part of this in his *Memoirs* I, pp. 348–49.

policy.[11] A lesser stylist could not get away with half Kennan's griping—and, truth to tell, even Kennan can grow tiresome on the subject. He offers a fine critique, as always, of democracy's weaknesses in the conduct of foreign affairs, but little of it is original and none of it is framed in such a way as to suggest practical improvements.

Some of Kennan's distaste for democracy looks like a distaste for the process of government in general. Much of what upsets him in the making of American foreign policy would no doubt be as true of the foreign policy process in Moscow or Peking or, for that matter, in Talleyrand's court. For Kennan's chief complaint is of "subjectivity":

> [M]ore important than the observable nature of external reality, when it comes to the determination of Washington's view of the world, is the subjective state of readiness on the part of Washington officialdom to recognize this or that feature of it. This is certainly natural: perhaps it is unavoidable. But it does raise the question—and it is a question which was to plague me increasingly over the course of the ensuing years— whether a government so constituted should deceive itself into believing that it is capable of conducting a mature, consistent, and discriminating foreign policy. Increasingly, with the years, my answer would tend to be in the negative.[12]

It seems to me that some fraction of this dissatisfaction can be dismissed as a yearning for the objective—a hopeless neatness and scientific exactitude—in foreign policy. This

---

[11]I would not wish to attempt a comprehensive list of references to this theme. Even a small fraction of them makes for a lengthy footnote: *American Diplomacy*, pp. 15–16, 22–23, 32–33, 36, 37, 55–56, 58–59, 65, 73, 74, 77–78; *Russia and the West*, pp. 5, 6, 135, 146, 147, 148–49, 223; *Memoirs* I, pp. 49, 50, 51, 52–53, 54, 185, 205, 295, 351, 413, 414; *Democracy and the Student Left*, pp. 184, 185, 186–87, 188–91, 204–5, 210–11, 223; *Memoirs* II, pp. 48, 144, 288, 292, 293–94, 297–98, 320–21, 322–23; *The Cloud of Danger*, pp. 4, 5, 6, 7, 8, 9–10, 11–26.

[12]Kennan, *Memoirs* I, p. 295.

yearning, which must always go unfulfilled, is the source of Kennan's diplomat-as-surgeon metaphors and the confusion of moral argument that I described in the last chapter. No government could satisfy him on this score.

Still, democracy, from the operational standpoint, seems especially calculated to offend Kennan.

First, there is the force of public opinion. It is simpleminded: "I am sure one could unite the American people," Kennan said recently, "and they would be capable of tremendous efforts; but, unfortunately, I can't see them uniting except on a primitive level of slogans and jingoistic ideological inspiration."[13] It is moody: "It is surely a curious characteristic of democracy: this amazing ability to shift gears overnight in one's ideological attitudes. . . ."[14] It is "subjective and emotional," lacking in "solemn and careful deliberation," even in decisions as serious as whether to go to war.[15] It is not even representative: "I suspect that what purports to be public opinion in most countries that consider themselves to have popular government is often not really the consensus of the feelings of the mass of the people at all but rather the expression of the interests of special highly vocal minorities. . . ."[16] It consequently undermines the ability of far-seeing statesmen to function: "One comes away from the reading of their [Woodrow Wilson's and Lloyd George's] experiences . . . with a question as to how much democracy was benefited by having men of such experience . . . since their impulses were so brutally negated by the opinion at home. . . ."[17]

Then there is Congress, especially with its expanded post-Watergate role in foreign affairs. It is clumsy: "[The division of powers] already goes far to rule out the privacy, the flexibility, and the promptness and incisiveness of

---

[13]Kennan and Urban, "A Conversation," p. 17.
[14]Kennan, *American Diplomacy*, p. 58.
[15]Ibid., p. 22.
[16]Ibid., p. 56.
[17]Kennan, *Russia and the West*, p. 148.

decision and action . . . which are generally considered necessary to the conduct of an effective world policy. . . ."[18] It is full of "dreary confusion": "Where others saw a stage on which momentous issues were being dramatically resolved, I saw only a sordid, never-ending Donnybrook among pampered and inflated egos; and I could never bring myself even to dare to hope that anything very constructive or very worthwhile might come out of it."[19] It is concerned above all with domestic politics: "The question, in these circumstances, became not: how effective is what I am doing in terms of the impact it makes on our world environment? but rather: how do I look, in the mirror of domestic American opinion, as I do it?"[20]

Kennan, as it sometimes seems, is torn between portraying congressmen as knowingly venal and pathetically ignorant. Occasionally he imputes a cynical, knowing recklessness to explain why Congress could do something so foolish as, for example, to cancel Yugoslavia's most-favored-nation trading status—"a gratuitous and studied slap at a smaller government against which, in our bilateral relations, we had no serious grievance." Kennan explains this, first, by crediting Congress with a desire to employ "chauvinist rhetoric, with which one demonstrated to the folks back home, on any and all occasions, that one was a hundred percent American. . . ." Yugoslavia, then, "was a target off which you could bounce your anti-Communist utterances with complete impunity, knowing that few people cared enough or knew enough about it to call you on the fine points."[21]

Most often, though, Kennan's congressmen (they are virtually never named) are merely stupid. Over that same issue of Yugoslavia, Kennan spent a week in the summer of 1962 lobbying on Capitol Hill. "The experience was an

---

[18]Kennan, *The Cloud of Danger*, p. 4.
[19]Kennan, *Memoirs* II, p. 322.
[20]Kennan, *Memoirs* I, p. 53.
[21]Kennan, *Memoirs* II, pp. 294, 288.

instructive one," he recalls, "inasmuch as it showed me, as nothing else ever had, the enormous gap in understanding and outlook that separated a person like myself from the likes of those I was talking with." Time after time, Kennan says, he found himself explaining to legislators that the question at issue was trade, not aid, and that trade was a mutual benefit: "Then there would be a moment of puzzled silence, after which the skeptical legislator would say something like this: 'Well, Mr. Ambassador, you may be right; but I still can't see why we have to go on giving aid to a lot of damned Communists.'"[22] One "distinguished member of the House of Representatives" actually had not heard that Yugoslavia was not a member of the Warsaw Pact, and said only, "Aw, go on," when Kennan so apprised him. "The unfeigned ignorance," Kennan writes, "was appalling."[23] Earlier in his career, Kennan recalls, he was required to seek an appointment with Stalin for a visiting delegation of congressmen. They were late, and some were drunk, when the time came for departure. In the limousine, one "raucous voice" demanded: "Who the hell is this guy Stalin, anyway? I don't know that I want to go up and see him. I think I'll get out." As this was not possible, the congressman settled back in his seat, only to come back again with: "What if I biff the old codger in the nose?"[24]

The whole notion of a separation of powers appears to be alien to Kennan:

> I pointed out that personally I had entered a profession which I thought had to do with the representation of United States interests vis-à-vis foreign governments; that this was what I had been trained for and what I was prepared to do to the best of my ability; and that I had

---

[22]Ibid., pp. 299–300. This attribution of anonymous buffoonery is one of the few cheap shots Kennan permits himself. Kennan's congressmen, it seems, scarcely speak a word without some mild profanity—a clear sign of Kennan's disapproval.

[23]Ibid., p. 285.

[24]Kennan, *Memoirs* I, p. 277.

never understood that part of my profession was to represent the US government vis-à-vis Congress; that my specialty was the defence of US interest against others, not against our own representatives; that I resented the State Department being put in the position of lobbyists before Congress in favor of the US people. . . .[25]

Again, when you believe in an objective national interest and believe you know what it is, it must be terribly offensive to see it battered about by charlatans and clowns in pursuit of their own domestic-political gain. Once you concede that the conduct of foreign affairs is subjective and entails choices among values, then the politics takes on a different veneer: individual legislators—even many legislators—may be charlatans and clowns, but the legislative process itself is necessary and legitimate. "Domestic politics" then must cease to be an all-purpose sneer—as in: "For obscure reasons of domestic politics . . . " or "the domestic-political aspects of these elaborate antics were not clear to me. . . ."[26]

Incredibly, Kennan came close to running for Congress himself in the early 1950s. As he tells it, a young farming couple knocked on his door at 146 Hodge Road in Princeton one evening and, without much in the way of preliminaries, asked him if he would consider a go at the candidacy in his home district in Pennsylvania. Kennan, "feeling it practically a civic duty to serve when one was asked in such a way to do so," said he was interested. What followed would be funny if Kennan were better suited to the role of *ingenue*. He discovered, to his horror, that running for office would deprive him of his income from the non-profit Institute for Advanced Studies and the Rockefeller Foundation. Then he discovered, worse still, that the Democrats who were backing him expected that he would approach the "local tycoons" for campaign funds, which he was "decidedly

---

[25]Diary, January 23, 1948, quoted in ibid., p. 405n.
[26]Ibid., pp. 458, 461.

disinclined to do." And so that was that. He withdrew from the race. Thus was southern Pennsylvania spared the questionable benefit of Kennan on Capitol Hill: long on contempt and despair of the antics around him, short on tolerance for the system of compromise and "courtesy" that is the lubricant of legislative life, Kennan would have been reduced very quickly to a regal and continuous dissent.[27]

In any case, it is not hard to see where all this talk of domestic politics is leading Kennan. The process of diplomacy, he sums up, "is marked by certain tragic contradictions": chief among which is that diplomats are employed by people to whom the "national interest" is not the main concern. "Their main concern is domestic politics; and the interests they find themselves pursuing in [this] field of activity are not only often but usually in conflict with the requirements of a sensible national diplomacy."

> [I]f . . . a considerable portion of a government's behavior is to remain effectively outside the control of those charged with shaping its policy in the national interest, and is going to be determined on the basis of motivations and purposes not necessarily related to the national interest at all, then that government may as well recognize that it is destined to move through the forest of international events like a man with some sort of muscular affliction, obliging him to perform purposeless and self-defeating movements. . . .[28]

Writing in 1951, Kennan maintained that history could not forgive America's foreign policy errors simply "because they are explicable in terms of our domestic politics." If *democracy* was causing the United States to make mistakes, he wrote, "let us recognize it and measure the full seriousness of it—and find something to do about it."[29] Kennan had

---

[27]Kennan, *Memoirs* II, pp. 77–80.
[28]Ibid., p. 319; *The Cloud of Danger*, p. 8.
[29]Kennan, *American Diplomacy*, p. 65.

by then all but decided that democracy *was*, in fact, the culprit. What he proposed to do about it was less clear.

III

On the issue of democratic government, as on most other issues, Kennan stresses the pragmatic over the theoretical. Some of his specific comments, however, suggest an underlying antipathy—or, at least, indifference—to the theoretical foundations of self-government, and that feeling makes for an important introduction to his thoughts on democratic reform.

Two examples help bring out the flavor of Kennan's idea of democracy. First, Kennan wrote in 1951 that it would be morally and politically justifiable to "outlaw" the American Communist Party, although he opposed such a step on prudential grounds.[30] Second, Kennan has more than once recalled that demonstrators in full Nazi regalia greeted Tito during his October, 1963, visit to Washington, and he confesses himself "unable to understand . . . to this day" why such a demonstration should have been "permitted." He writes: "I puzzle . . . over the question of what is wrong with the outlooks and habits of a great country which professes itself unable to assure to the personal guest of its own President, so long as that guest is on its territory, immunity from the most disgusting sort of insult and harassment."[31] Nowhere does Kennan mention that the United States Constitution is usually thought to preclude the banning of a political party; or that even the president himself, let alone his "guest," lacks immunity from the sometimes unpleasant manifestations of free political expression. He does not bother to indicate that he under-

---

[30]Kennan, "Where Do You Stand On Communism?" *The New York Times Magazine*, May 27, 1951. Kennan appears to endorse this position in *Memoirs* II, p. 198.

[31]Kennan, *Memoirs* II, pp. 314, 315. See also Severeid interview, side B.

stands, still less agrees with, the fundamental rationale for permitting Communists and extremists to annoy and frustrate responsible officials.

In general, Kennan sees democracy as a cultural and historical arrangement, the product of unique circumstances, and he denies vigorously that "'democracy,' or what we picture to ourselves under that word, is the natural state of most of mankind." It can extend, he says, "only to people of our own kind," by which he means that

> the capability for effective self-government seems to me to be pretty well restricted to countries that satisfy one of two requirements: small size and cultural cohesion, and particularly, for some reason, to those that border on the English Channel and the North Sea or have taken their origins from these coastal states. I do not claim this to be a form of superiority; you may say that these Northern nations have been more fortunate in some ways than their Southern neighbors. Whatever the reason, it is a fact that democracy is not widespread or successful beyond this northern tier of Europe. . . . The taste (what the French call *goût*) for democracy is geographically and historically limited.[32]

This view not only is questionable in its application to India and Israel,[33] but it seems to confuse the empirical for the abstract. There is no shortage of argument about why the consent of the governed should be a moral prerequisite for government—I certainly will not try to rehearse it all here—and yet Kennan insists on evading this philosophical issue in favor of an observation that is at best irrelevant and

---

[32]Kennan, *The Cloud of Danger*, p. 41; *American Diplomacy*, p. 22; Kennan and Urban, "A Conversation," pp. 30–31.

[33]If it is argued that these two nations "have taken their origins" from the coastal cradle of democracy, then a great proportion of the rest of the world's nations must have similar origins. Few states have escaped Europe's imperial touch. If it is argued that India and Israel do not have "democracy," then the definition of democracy must be very narrow indeed.

at worst incorrect. Democracy is not only a descriptive term; it is also the expression of a political ideal. Kennan's support for this ideal is ambivalent at best, and his ambivalence should be kept firmly in mind when reading his practical ideas for reform.

At first, during the cautiously optimistic year at the War College, Kennan saw democratic reform as a simple—if not politically easy—matter. Three steps would go a long way toward solving America's problems of coherence and coordination in foreign affairs: first, a "more effective liaison between the Executive and Congress"; second, "a little better indoctrination of the American public"; and third, "more sheer courage in government . . . before domestic criticism."[34] This last step was to become increasingly important to Kennan as his optimism regarding the first two grew to fade. Kennan's point, recalling Edmund Burke, was that a government owed the people its judgment as well as its allegiance. As the years passed, he would be more and more inclined to counsel that the government simply ignore mistaken public and congressional opinion.

This theme came out explicitly—in an off-the-record talk—as early as 1946. An officer student at the National War College asked Kennan how America could achieve consistency in foreign policy. Kennan first urged a better effort at "making [government] policies understandable to the people," but then he added that the people would nonetheless sometimes fail to understand:

> This is a dangerous subject to discuss publicly. I see no reason why we shouldn't face it frankly here. . . . I think we would be very poor representatives of our country indeed if we were to sit back passively, knowing all we know, and say: "Our own views don't come into the question, and we do just what the people tell us to." . . . The government has got to insist on what it believes is

---

[34]"Russia," Naval War College lecture, October 1, 1946, *Kennan Papers*, Box 16.

right and go right ahead with it. . . . There is no use electing people and then ham-stringing them day after day by criticism.[35]

Evidently, Kennan also hoped and expected that the widespread appreciation of a Soviet threat in the late 1940s would galvanize American opinion and instill a new sense of purpose in government leaders. The reality of Soviet power, he wrote, is "not only the greatest and most complex of our present problems of national policy but represents unquestionably the greatest test of statesmanship that our country has ever faced."[36] Similar sentiments had also appeared prominently in the X-Article, in which Kennan called Soviet–American competition "in essence a test of the over-all worth of the United States as a nation among nations," and added: "To avoid destruction the United States need only measure up to its own best traditions and prove itself worthy of preservation as a great nation." He left little doubt as to his own belief on the outcome:

Surely, there was never a fairer test of national quality than this. In the light of these circumstances, the thoughtful observer of Russian–American relations will find no cause for complaint in the Kremlin's challenge to American society. He will rather experience a certain gratitude to a Providence which, by providing the American people with this implacable challenge, has made their entire security as a nation dependent on their pulling themselves together and accepting the responsibility of moral and political leadership that history plainly intended them to bear.[37]

"If it [the Soviet threat] had never existed," Kennan later quoted a colleague as saying, "we would have had to invent

---

[35]Question-and-answer period, NWC lecture, September 16, 1946, *Kennan Papers*, Box 16.
[36]Kennan, *Realities of American Foreign Policy*, p. 63.
[37][Kennan], "The Sources of Soviet Conduct," p. 582.

it, to create the sense of urgency we need to bring us to the point of decisive action."[38]

Walter Lippmann, in the third of twelve columns responding to the X-Article, argued that "Americans would themselves probably be frustrated by Mr. X's policy long before the Russians were."[39] Kennan did not immediately agree with this view, but he came to be convinced of it later. Sometime in the early 1950s, so far as can be determined from the incomplete published record, Kennan by degrees lost all faith in the potential coherence and good sense of American public opinion.

For a long while, this loss of faith left Kennan with little more than his frequent and largely futile pleas for greater reliance on "professionals" to conceive and execute foreign policy.[40] "To Kennan's way of thinking," Rostow snickers, "the conduct of foreign affairs is a technical matter that should be left to the experts—that is, to the professionals. They know best. The President can be allowed some supervisory jurisdiction, but not much. And Congress should be kept in its place altogether."[41] Like most of Rostow's article, this swipe distorts Kennan but also contains a kernel of truth. By 1957, Kennan was uncomfortably close to arguing that the "unavoidable gap between specialized knowledge and public understanding" precludes any useful role for the public in the formation of foreign policy:

> . . . I am reluctant to cross that crucial border beyond which one *admits* that foreign affairs are exclusively the province of the full-time professional, in which the views of the private citizen can have no value. *Even if this were largely so*, the admission of it would carry us

---

[38]NWC lecture, "Where Do We Stand?" December 21, 1949, *Kennan Papers*, Box 17.

[39]Lippmann, *The Cold War*, p. 20.

[40]See, for example, *American Diplomacy*, p. 81; *Realities of American Foreign Policy*, pp. 95–96; *Russia, the Atom and the West*, pp. vii–viii; *Memoirs I*, pp. 74, 82–83, 115, 139–40.

[41]Rostow, "Searching for Kennan's Grand Design."

into a new range of political realities for which neither our political systems nor our habits of thought are prepared.[42]

Kennan was in a bind: he felt that the government desperately needed change, and yet he could not quite envision what that change should be.

The direction, at least, was clear: America needed discipline, spiritual authority, a sense of purpose. In the last of his prewar despatches from Prague, Kennan had speculated about the political future of Czechoslovakia if it succeeded in freeing itself from (at the time) German hegemony:

> [T]hat the Czechs will ever restore in full their past institutions and their past leaders is doubtful. Misfortune has left many marks; and among them is a deep sense of the necessity for unity and discipline. . . . Few will wish for the return of the many squabbling political parties, the petty-bourgeois timidity, and the shallow materialism which seems to have characterized at least the lower organs of public administration under the former regime. Czech nationalism will flourish indeed, but with it there will be a demand for greater personal responsibility and greater spiritual authority among those who pretend to lead.[43]

Outstanding in this passage is the suggestion that democracy is, as he has argued morality is, something of a luxury and—very often—something of a pretense.

Leadership, which is truly of the essence, could only come from an elite. In 1975, Eric Severeid asked Kennan what he made of accusations that he wanted to run foreign policy in some sort of "priestly cult." Kennan did not quite deny the charge:

---

[42]Kennan, *Russia, the Atom and the West*, pp. vii–viii [emphasis added].

[43]Despatch of August 19, 1939, reprinted in *From Prague After Munich: Diplomatic Papers, 1938–1940* (Princeton: Princeton University Press, 1968), p. 224. See also *American Diplomacy*, pp. 110–11; *Memoirs I*, p. 104.

> I am . . . anything but an egalitarian. I am very much
> opposed to egalitarian tendencies of all sorts in gov-
> ernmental life and in other walks of life. Sometimes I've
> been charged with being an elitist. Of *course* I am. What
> do people expect? God forbid that we should be without
> an elite. Is everything to be done by gray mediocrity?
> After all, our whole system is based on the selection of
> people for different functions in our life, and when you
> talk about selection you're talking about an elite.[44]

Sereveid did not follow up on this, which is a shame. After
all, probably not since Lenin's *State and Revolution* has
anyone seriously argued that government can be run
without an elite. The real question is of that elite's responsibility to and ultimate sanction in mass political opinion.

Actually, Severeid's "priestly cult" metaphor was better
than he knew. For Kennan, by his own account, was
profoundly influenced by the famous "Grand Inquisitor"
chapter of Dostoevsky's *The Brothers Karamazov*. Dostoevsky,
in a parable, portrayed the dilemma faced by an aging
cardinal in the Roman Catholic Inquisition: he believed in
Christ's way, but he knew that only an elect few would truly
follow it. The very freedom of moral choice meant that many
would reject Christ; and yet to take away men's freedom in
the name of Christ would do violence to Christianity. This
was the dilemma of the Inquisition—it might make "believ-
ers" out of all who survived, but in so doing it would violate
the beliefs themselves. Kennan saw a parallel in politics:

> Dilemmas produce agony; and the agony of this one
> came in the form of the first reluctant and horrifying
> pangs of doubt as to whether America's problems were
> really soluble at all by operation of the liberal-
> democratic and free-enterprise institutions traditional to
> our country. . . .
> What did this mean? Did it mean that [Commun-
> ists], fundamentally, were right and we—wrong? That

---

[44]Severeid interview, side B.

modern man in the mass had to be thought of as a lost and blinded child who could be led out of his dangers and bewilderments only by bold, ruthless, self-confident minorities, armed with insights higher than any of which the masses were to be presumed capable. . . ?[45]

Dostoevsky's Grand Inquisitor wound up choosing the path of coercion. Kennan, however much he deplores the results of freedom, never had any interest in doing the same. But that did not stop him, in the decade of the 1970s, from seeking a "middle ground" between the two choices.

In a lonely and mysterious sentence, buried deep in an article in 1970, Kennan wrote simply, "The Constitution needs revision."[46] Kennan appears to have been attracted for a time to the idea of regional government, believing that America is too big and spread out to support an efficient representative system. Whatever his program, he hinted often that he would like to see Constitutional change.[47] He elaborated at length for the first time, so far as I could discover, in the Urban interview of 1975:

> I can see no reason why a popular control of government should be inconsistent with forceful and purposeful government if the institutions of government are properly designed. . . . [W]e ought to create a panel, or pool of outstanding people, that would comprise perhaps 500–1000 souls. Appointment to it would be by some detached and austere authority such as the Supreme Court, and membership in it would represent recognition of distinction in our national life achieved by a man's own efforts outside the field of political competition. One could then say to the electorate: "You

---

[45]Kennan, *Memoirs* II, pp. 85–86. See also Kennan and Urban, "A Conversation," p. 29; *Democracy and the Student Left*, p. 12.

[46]Kennan, "Con III Is Not The Answer," *The New York Times*, October 18, 1970.

[47]See, for example, *Democracy and the Student Left*, pp. 16, 234–36.

can nominate people for election to the Senate—but
only from among this body."

. . . I am talking of a "meritocracy" which we do
have plentifully in this country, but are failing to use
properly.

And later in the interview:

Let me repeat that the first requirement is a system of
selection of an elite which is not based on false values,
which really does recognize merit both of the intellect
and of character and responsibility. The people who
have these qualities have to be encouraged and brought
to a point where they can be seen and recognized, and
then given responsibility. I don't think they should be
given it indefinitely—one must have an occasional
appeal to the public for a vote of confidence.[48]

Urban, by this point somewhat skeptical, asked, "Isn't
your plea for the acceptance of an intellectual aristocracy a
very difficult one in a basically egalitarian society?" Kennan
replied: "Surely, one should be content with a modest
station in life if one has modest capabilities." Kennan
emphasized that "I don't want to see any dictatorship set up
in this country, and I would not want to be part of one if it
were." But he had not even the vaguest suggestion of how
his meritocracy, legitimated by an occasional, tasteful appeal
to the public, could conceivably come into being otherwise
than by coercion.[49]

It is hard to decide what to make of all this. H. L.
Mencken might simply snort and call it "flumdiddle." Civil
libertarians might call it—have called it—pernicious and
antidemocratic. In truth, it is a little of both. Kennan himself
records that his friends most often reacted to his views on
government with "indulgent smiles and kindly observations
to the effect that I didn't really know anything about the

---

[48]Kennan and Urban, "A Conversation," pp. 28, 32.
[49]Ibid., pp. 33, 32.

United States and had better stick to my real *métier*, which was foreign affairs."[50] Perhaps this is, after all, the best way to respond. It does no good to beat Kennan about the head with Locke, Mill, and *The Federalist*. He is doing little more, it seems, than venting his frustration.

The problem with this sort of steam-letting, when one is George Kennan, is that it leaves one open to simple-minded criticism. Kennan sounds silly when he talks prescriptively about democracy—sets himself up for Rostow's sneers—and to no good end at all. For he really does understand the dilemma of all attempts to "discipline" a democracy:

> Every legislative body is in many respects an evil; but it is a necessary one. It provides worse government, unquestionably, than does a benevolent despotism. But it provides better government than the non-benevolent despotism into which the benevolent one has a tendency eventually to evolve. The parliamentary institution, imperfect as it is, stands as a wholly indispensable link beween the will of the people and the execution of supreme governmental authority.[51]

Kennan's valid and important criticisms of democracy are just too easy to dismiss when he insists on accompanying them with suggestions for change that can hardly be described as other than half-baked.

IV

In the end, Kennan is realist enough to have decided by now on the futility of his "meritocratic" course—though perhaps not entirely out of abstract conviction. Change simply will not happen that way. And besides, Kennan does have a

---

[50]Kennan, *Memoirs* II, p. 88.
[51]Kennan, *Democracy and the Student Left*, pp. 206–7.

curious love–hate relationship with democracy. He dwells on the negative, but his grudging respect is no less real for its infrequent expression. And so in 1977 he wrote:

> I can well conceive that the way this country is now governed is substantially the only way a country of our size and extent *could* be governed, if one is to hold to democratic principles. It should come as no surprise to anyone to be reminded that there are always prices to be paid for democratic liberties.

The "prices" in this case are all the inefficiencies and confusions that Kennan has written so much about. "My plea is only that . . . the implications of this state of affairs for America's performance as a participant in world politics should be recognized, and the attendant lessons taken into account." Earlier in this chapter, I quoted Kennan as saying that America is "like a man with some sort of muscular affliction"; Kennan's advice, therefore, is that the government should "avoid getting into games which call for the utmost coordination and control of muscular power."[52]

There is none of Churchill's high spirit in this final, reluctant concession to democracy as the best alternative. Kennan is little more than resigned, almost spellbound by a sense of limits. He has spent too much of his life declaiming against the political system to keep up his hopes in the absence of structural change. And that is sad.

As always after reading Kennan awhile, I have an overwhelming impulse to say: *yes, but.* Yes, democracy is a messy and unwieldy process, but it is perhaps not so helpless as Kennan conceives it. Yes, the United States often behaves like a man with a muscular affliction, but the cure is not in giving up hope of coordination, nor is it in the sort of radical surgery and bulky prosthetics that Kennan prescribed in the 1970s.

---

[52]Kennan, *The Cloud of Danger*, pp. 7–8.

The problem—the real, root problem—with Kennan's pessimism about democracy is that it leads inexorably, with something like logic, to the strategic fallacies discussed in Chapter 2 and the moral standoffishness discussed in Chapter 3. Since Kennan believes America incapable of a coherent global policy, he must try to contrive some "indispensable minimum" perimeter of interests, even though the War College Kennan would concede that such a perimeter—as a rigid guide to policy—can make no strategic sense. And he must reject moral standards in the conduct of foreign affairs, even though he is a deeply moral man and cannot resist espousing values in the end.

Kennan emphasizes the unanswerable when he talks of democracy's incoherence, but he can be answered nonetheless, and on his own terms: the best is enemy of the good.[53] It seems a strange fault in a self-described realist, but Kennan is judging a stubbornly unregenerate world by ideal standards—ideal efficiency, ideal integrity, ideal wisdom. Certainly the United States should cut back on wasteful and far-flung commitments; certainly it should shy off from simplistic moralism; certainly it should recognize the limits of coherence in the democratic process. But it should above all be striving to overcome those limits and behave as if it means to remain a great and positive force in world affairs. Kennan was closer to an answer in 1946, when he called on government to consolidate its policy, make the best case it can to the public, and then ride out the criticism that will always eventually come. On that path, and on that path only, lies hope.

---

[53]Kennan says this often, but usually in French: *le mieux est l'ennemi du bien*. See *Memoirs* II, pp. 141, 350; *Democracy and the Student Left*, p. 170.

IV

THE POTENTIAL OF POWER

FIVE

On Tactics
and the Tools of Power

> [W]e must be gardeners and not mechanics in our approach to world affairs. . . . The forces of nature will generally be on the side of him who understands them best and respects them most scrupulously.
>
> *Kennan*

If Kennan had set out deliberately to obfuscate, he could have improved very little on the bewilderment that has greeted his views on the tactics and tools of American power in world affairs. Nowhere is Kennan more often—or more wrongly—accused of contradicting himself than on the role of military force in international life, and on no other issue, surely, is he less often understood. There is no obvious reason for all the confusion, because although Kennan is never a model of systematic expression, his views on the relation of war to politics are coherent and substantially consistent over time. But confusion there is, and much of the dreary and interminable disputation over "containment" and the X-Article turns on just this question of what is "political" as distinct from "military" power—and specifically, what Kennan meant by "counter-force" in the context of Soviet-American relations.

I do not hope to settle this argument once and for all, but I have satisfied myself at least as to what containment was *not*. It was not, as has commonly been supposed, primarily a military doctrine,[1] nor merely a passive and reactive tactical plan,[2] nor, as Kennan seems to claim in his *Memoirs*, a scheme purely for "the political containment of a political threat"[3]—at least not as "political" is generally understood. Meanwhile, along the way to understanding the tactics of containment, I must sketch in what is just as important: Kennan's broader views on the tools of power available to the United States.

I

If a nation's means of influence in foreign affairs were conceived as a spectrum, that spectrum would start, pleasantly enough, with gestures of friendship and favor, and then continue through negotiation and various forms of pressure to the opposite end: all-out war. Kennan has dedicated much of his writing career to the proposition that—at least since World War I—all-out war has ceased to be a coherent means to any desirable end. "Modern war is not just an instrument of policy," Kennan told his BBC audience in 1957.

---

[1]See Lippmann, *The Cold War*; Wright, "Mr. 'X' and Containment"; Mark, "What Kind of Containment?"

[2]See James Burnham, *Containment or Liberation? An Inquiry into the Aims of United States Foreign Policy* (New York: The John Day Company, 1952). Part One, pp. 13–76.

[3]Kennan, *Memoirs* I, p. 358.

It is an experience in itself. It does things to him who practices it, irrespective of whether he wins or loses. . . . Let us by all means think for once not just in the mathematics of destruction—not just in these grisly equations of probable military casualties—let us rather think of people as they are; of the limits of their strength, their hope, their capacity for suffering, their capacity for believing in the future. And let us ask ourselves in all seriousness how much worth saving is going to be saved if war now rages for the third time in a half-century over the face of Europe. . . .[4]

By the start of the twentieth century, Kennan said in an Oxford lecture, it should have been apparent that "prolonged warfare in the industrial age, with its fearful expenditure of blood and substance, was bound to be self-defeating. . . . In other words, it did not take the atom to make warfare with modern weapons a fruitless and self-defeating exercise."[5] The industrial revolution had vastly— exponentially—increased man's capacity for destruction: the machine gun and explosive artillery shell, and later the airplane, submarine, and guided missile, had rendered war so frightfully powerful a force that it could no longer be controlled once fully unleashed. Few could realize this, Kennan writes, in the nineteenth century:

It was not understood that there could be genetic losses of such seriousness that they could not be made good by any conceivable fruits of victory—impermanent, shifting, steadily yielding to the sands of time as all these fruits were bound to be. It was not understood that the anguish of modern war could weaken even the ostensibly victorious society, breaking the rhythm of the generations, loosening social bonds, brutalizing sensibilities, sowing sadness, bewilderment, and skepticism where once the opposites of those qualities had pre-

---

[4]Kennan, *Russia, the Atom and the West*, pp. 58–59.
[5]Kennan, *Russia and the West*, p. 9.

vailed. . . . It was not understood, in other words, that all-out war between great industrialized nations in the modern age had become a senseless undertaking, a self-destructive exercise, a game at which no one could really win, and therefore no longer a suitable instrument of national policy.[6]

By 1946, when Kennan took on his War College duties, he was sure that this view of all-out war was beyond dispute.[7]

The recognition of war's unacceptable levels of destruction led logically to a corollary: "[J]ust because you have an enemy, and recognize him as such, does not necessarily mean that you are obliged to destroy him or can afford the luxury of all-out attempts to do so."[8] It also led to a view of nuclear weapons that put Kennan at odds with more than three decades of official American doctrine on war. "Even the tactical atomic weapon," Kennan wrote, "is destructive to a degree that sickens the imagination." Nuclear weapons took the same place in Kennan's thought as all-out war: there was no positive use for either of them. "[T]he weapon of mass destruction," Kennan wrote, "is a sterile and hopeless weapon . . . which cannot in any way serve the purposes of a constructive and hopeful foreign policy." It is "unsuitable . . . as a sanction of diplomacy." Kennan's views on nuclear weapons would fill a chapter in themselves, but I should say this much here: Kennan is unalterably opposed to any doctrine calling for "first use," or the use other than in retaliation, of nuclear weapons; he doubts that marginal changes in the nuclear "balance" are meaningful; and he does not believe that the threat to use nuclear weapons

---

[6]Kennan, *The Decline of Bismarck's European Order*, p. 423.

[7]See, for example, ibid., p. 424; *Russia and the West*, pp. 32, 179, 201, 391; *American Diplomacy*, pp. 50–56. Oddly, there is little of this sentiment stated explicitly in Kennan's unpublished papers of 1946 to 1949, perhaps because Kennan felt it unnecessary to belabor it in light of America's war-weariness and rapid demobilization.

[8]Kennan, *Russia and the West*, p. 177.

against another state can be turned to a nation's political advantage.[9]

With all this, Kennan seems to be firmly taking sides in an ongoing debate over the nature of thermonuclear force. Is the Bomb some wholly new creation, something different in kind from all weapons that have gone before, or is it merely a grossly magnified club for use against one's enemies? Despite his comparisons of the nuclear weapon with all-out war, Kennan most often takes the former view. Since he has lived through and contributed to the strategic nuclear debate from its beginnings, a brief review provides useful context here.

The power of fission (and now fusion) revealed itself almost immediately as a paradox. Pegged "the absolute weapon" within a year of its first and only use, the atom bomb tends to present itself at first sight as a unique and overwhelming phenomenon, transcending and even rendering irrelevant any traditional notion of the balance of power. Against this reflexive gasp has arisen, since the early 1950s, a bulky strategic literature which places the atom squarely back in the continuum of military might and which tends to deny that nuclear weapons are unique in any important way as a projection of national power. Much can be said for this hardheaded willingness to confront the nuclear issue. But it has seemed to Kennan, rightly, I think, that the rush for the slide rules has obscured some of the valuable insights of that first reflexive gasp.

For the "strategic realists," there are a number of points. A nuclear weapon, first of all, is an instrument of destruction, and in that sense is like other tools of war, only more so. "Against defenseless people," to use Thomas Schelling's deliberately gruesome image, "there is not much that nuclear

---

[9]Kennan, *Russia, the Atom and the West*, pp. 55, 58–59; *The Cloud of Danger*, p. 125; *Memoirs I*, p. 311; *Realities of American Foreign Policy*, pp. 84–85; Kennan and Urban, "A Conversation," p. 59. An extremely useful compilation is George F. Kennan, *The Nuclear Delusion: Soviet–American Relations in the Atomic Age* (New York: Pantheon, 1982).

weapons can do that cannot be done with an ice pick."[10] In this way, nuclear weaponry is seen as merely one—albeit potent—ingredient of national power. And if it is difficult to find a common conversion point between "conventional" and "nuclear" military potential (how many tanks equal an ICBM?) it may be no easier to weigh economic or ideological power with military power, all on the same scale. This is a problem with the concept of "balance of power" itself. Yet strategists do, in the end, have to assess national power in the aggregate.

Even those who believe that the nuclear weapon is nothing radically new usually concede certain differences with prior armaments. Many strategists believe, for example, that mutual nuclear deterrence requires only some high threshold of threatened damage in order to work, not actual equality of forces. This is because victory is no prerequisite for inflicting unacceptable damage with nuclear weapons: the increments and range of destruction available even to a lesser power are staggering. Also, whereas a conventional balance of power is essentially an objective matter, because easily tested at the margins, mutual nuclear deterrence is a highly subjective and psychological affair. And whereas the classical balance of power seeks first of all to preserve the international system, even at the sometime expense of peace, mutual nuclear deterrence seeks to preserve peace itself first of all.

These are significant points, but Kennan's is more basic. He is simply unwilling to be drawn into the strategic debate, with all its talk of game theory and "throw-weights" and "circular error probability" and "radius of destruction." Even to begin the discussion in technical terms, Kennan believes, is to lose all hope of talking sense about nuclear weapons. The idea to keep firmly in mind, rather, is that it makes no sense to contemplate using these arms, and therefore that it makes no sense to manufacture and stockpile them by the

---

[10]Thomas Schelling, *Arms and Influence* (New Haven: Yale University Press, 1966), p. 19.

tens of thousands of megatons. There is both more and less to this argument than meets the eye.

Its merits are in some ways intuitive and obvious, but it is helpful here to return to the raw conception of power in international affairs. Power is usefully defined as the ability to achieve intended results, and a balance of power, classically, is defined in the negative: no nation has a preponderance that permits it to lay down the law to others. The question arises: in what sense could the power of nuclear arms possibly lead to this sort of preponderance? What Kennan argues is that destructive nuclear power can lead to no sane intentional result. It is implausible as an instrument of coercion, simply on account of its scale. In real life, nations do not try, say, to compel other nations to change their tariff structures or even to withdraw behind certain boundaries by nuking a city if they fail to comply. Kennan believes, after Stalin, that nuclear weapons are largely idle threats with which to frighten people with weak nerves. What conventional military force can do, and the nuclear weapon cannot, is to create political facts: it can occupy territory, police it, organize it under authority, compel and prevent actions on an ordinary human scale. Nuclear weapons can only obliterate, and on a scale that can serve few useful ends.

To illustrate Kennan's point, does anyone imagine that nuclear "preponderance" did the United States any good in the hostage affair with Iran? Conventional force, in theory, might have freed the hostages, or, on a much greater scale, imposed a new government on Iran. Nuclear force could have had nothing to say about any such coercive objectives. Even in situations of active hostility, the nuclear weapon is of dubious value. Once in Korea, twice in Vietnam (once each for the United States and China), once very recently in the Falkland Islands, and now, arguably, in Afghanistan, a nuclear power has fought a have-not on the have-not's own terms—not only without recourse to nuclear weapons, but with nuclear weapons so far in the political background as to be just about out of sight. The reason seems unlikely to be that all the nuclear powers were insufficiently ruthless. In fact, there was dark talk in more than one of these cases of the possibility of nuclear attack. If the talk had no impact, it is because such threats are not only incredible, but incoherent.

Rather than one among many ingredients of national power, nuclear force seems to be almost entirely self-referential—good for little but deterring a like force of somebody else's. Even the idea of "extended" deterrence—that Western Europe has been spared a conventional invasion only by the American nuclear guarantee—is counterfactual. That is, the nuclear umbrella cannot be proved (or disproved) to have been the operating factor. At best, then, nuclear weapons exert a peculiar form of negative influence on workaday world affairs.

None of this (and in following the spirit of Kennan's argument I have added to the letter) is to argue that nuclear weapons are irrelevant. They are merely different. In many ways they *are* the absolute weapon, and to quote Schelling once more, "There is a simplicity, a kind of virginity, about all-or-none distinctions that differences of degree do not have."[11] In other words, it seems almost reasonable to divide power into two sorts: nuclear, and all other. They rarely meet. In most of the business of international life, the balance of power depends on conventional military, economic, and ideological influence. The thousands of warheads of potential nuclear destruction, left out of this everyday world, await silently in their silos and maneuver largely in the subjective, shadowy, virginal realm reserved for themselves alone.

At this point in the argument, Kennan tends to grow impatient, and he tries to sound as though it follows that nuclear weapons are simply dispensable public hazards. In his imagined address to Soviet and American leaders, from which I have quoted once before, he says: "No one should wish to have in his hands such powers. Thrust them from

---

[11]Ibid., p. 132.

you."[12] This could be permitted as rhetorical, but it is not entirely so. In a hundred indirect ways, Kennan verges on asserting that mutual disarmament is simply a matter of willing it. He cannot understand or forgive the dynamics of the arms race. He loses his historian's detachment. His tone ranges from the hortatory to the cynical, as if only moral blindness or narrow self-interest could inhibit Soviet and American leaders from disarmament.

In thinking about nuclear arms, Kennan could usefully give more attention to game theory, and in particular to the theory of "non-zero-sum, non-cooperative games." The well-known game of Prisoner's Dilemma, which has powerful implications for the arms race, is of this sort. Its classical form is as follows: Two prisoners, known (without proof) to be guilty of a serious crime, are informed by the prosecutor that each of them individually must choose whether or not to confess. If neither confesses, the prosecutor can only convict them of a lesser crime. If both confess, the prosecutor promises not to seek the maximum penalty. If only one of them confesses (implicating the other), he will be granted immunity and the other will face a sentence of death. Each prisoner individually would be best off if he confessed and the other did not; jointly, they would be best off if neither confessed; but in fact the outcome of the game seems sure to be that both confess and both suffer long prison terms. *Even if they are permitted to negotiate*, neither can trust the other absolutely not to break his vow of silence, and neither will be willing to risk his life on the likelihood. It has often been argued that the position of the United States and the Soviet Union in arms control talks uncomfortably resembles that of the prisoners. "Verifiability" of arms control agreements is always a crucial and difficult issue for precisely this reason. It helps nothing for Kennan to point out that both sides have a common interest in arms control and to urge that they quit worrying and simply do it.

---

[12]See p. 77.

Again, I believe Kennan refuses any part in the technical aspects of the discussion for fear of the thin edge of the wedge: once he lets in the idiom of the strategists, he cannot see how to control it. And it is true—the language and concepts of nuclear strategy have a seductive internal logic. Those who think arms control a fantasy are likewise blinded, by this same internal logic, to the insights of critics like Kennan. The partisans are talking past each other. All this is understandable, but a pity. Kennan might well have a statesmanlike contribution to make if he learned to speak the language of the other side.

II

Kennan's persuasive point, which applies equally to nuclear and other forms of mass destruction, was that all-out war no longer could be useful as a policy instrument. With that in mind, Kennan decided in 1946 that Americans would have to rethink their traditional approach to the use of military force:

> The precedents of our Civil War, of the war with Spain, and of our participation in the two world wars of this century, had created not only in the minds of our soldiers and sailors but in the minds of many of our people an unspoken assumption that the normal objective of warfare was the total destruction of the enemy's ability and will to resist and his unconditional capitulation. The rest, it was always assumed, was easy. . . .
>
> The most significant of the appreciations to which I came during that year at the War College was that this approach to the cultivation and use by our country of armed forces would no longer work.[13]

---

[13]Kennan, *Memoirs* I, pp. 309–10.

If there was to be a continued role for the use of military force in American foreign policy, the United States would have to evolve a concept of *limited* warfare—"warfare conducted for limited objectives and ending with the achievement of those objectives by compromise with the existing enemy regime. . . ."[14]

Kennan should not be mistaken for a pacifist. "Such is the stubbornness and recalcitrance of human nature," he wrote in 1964, "that the use of force cannot always be foreign to the process of persuasion." But, on the other hand: "[W]ar has to have an object. There have to be war aims. If you conduct military operations, you have to be willing to state what you would settle for." And that object, those war aims, the *what* you would settle for, have to be limited—because total capitulation can be had only by total war. Americans have to accept instead "the very narrow and limited degree to which force can ever be the main solution for problems that involve the states of mind—the outlooks and convictions—of great masses of people on this planet."[15] Ten years earlier, Kennan had made much the same point in his Stafford Little Lecture Series at Princeton: "People have become accustomed to saying that the day of limited wars is over. I would submit that the truth is exactly the opposite: that the day of total wars has passed, and that from now on limited military operations are the only ones that could conceivably serve any coherent purpose."[16]

These reflections on the uses of military power led Kennan to a concept of the peacetime requirements of American armed forces that emphasized "small mobile

---

[14]Kennan, *Memoirs II*, p. 95.

[15]Kennan, *On Dealing with the Communist World* (New York: Harper & Row, 1964), pp. 15, 18.

[16]Kennan, *Realities of American Foreign Policy*, p. 80. Elsewhere Kennan writes: "If weapons were to be used at all, they would have to be employed to temper the ambitions of an adversary, or to make good limited objectives against his will—not to destroy his power, or his government, or to disarm him entirely" (*Memoirs I*, p. 310).

forces" in constant, alert readiness and the maintenance of a capability "to mobilize our strength rapidly if a clear threat of major war developed." Kennan felt, in 1947, that the United States should

> maintain what we may call an adequate military posture: a posture of quiet strength and alertness combined with patience and dignity, a posture which will make it unmistakably evident that this nation has the strength to back up its convictions if necessary and which will relieve any would-be aggressors abroad of any hopeful delusions that their schemes would be abetted by a lack of preparedness or vigilance on our part. . . . If we are not willing to meet this obligation, we have no business to ask for the things we are asking for in international life or to hope that another world catastrophe can be avoided.

Kennan's "quiet strength" was meant to be something of a precision instrument, suited to small-scale and short-notice applications of force:

> We must remember that the first line of American defense might be many thousands of miles from American shores. We already hold a number of outlying bases . . . and it might be necessary for us on very short notice to seize and hold other . . . outlying island bases or peninsular bases on other continents, if only for the purpose of denying the use of them to others during the period required for further military preparations. But here, again . . . the greatest value of our forces lies in their quality as a deterrent. If we do not maintain such forces there will always be an incentive to unruly people elsewhere to seize isolated and limited objectives on the theory that we would be able to do nothing about it at the moment and that they could count on making the seizures with impunity and talking about it afterward. . . .

Kennan, as these passages show, had a tendency sometimes to talk tough—in the abstract.[17]

But he soon came to believe that the rational and limited use of armed forces, as opposed to their maintenance as a deterrent, was difficult in the extreme for a democracy. It was not only the military chain of command that was "addicted to doing things only in the most massive, ponderous and unwieldy manner"[18]—it was also the American public. "A democracy," Kennan wrote in his private notes in 1948, "is severely restricted in the use of armed forces as a weapon of peacetime foreign policy. It cannot use them as an offensive threat. It cannot manipulate them tactically, on any extensive scale, for the accomplishment of measures short of war. . . ."[19] The reason? A democracy, bedeviled by emotionalism and whimsy, was capable of fighting only one way: "It soon becomes the victim of its own war propaganda. It then tends to attach to its own cause an absolute value, which distorts its own vision on everything else. *Its* enemy becomes the embodiment of all evil. *Its* own side, on the other hand, is the center of all virtue."[20]

> This lends to the democratic war effort a basically punitive note, rather than one of expediency. I mention this because, if there is anything in this thought, it goes far to explain the difficulty we have in employing force for rational and restricted purposes rather than for purposes which are emotional and to which it is hard to find a rational limit.[21]

---

[17]Kennan, "Requirements of National Security," talk to the National Defense Committee, Chamber of Commerce of the United States, January 23, 1947, *Kennan Papers*, Box 16.

[18]Kennan, *Memoirs* II, p. 52.

[19]Private paper, "Comments on the General Trend of U.S. Foreign Policy," August 20, 1948, *Kennan Papers*, Box 23.

[20]Kennan, *Russia and the West*, p. 5 [emphasis in original].

[21]Kennan, *American Diplomacy*, pp. 73–74.

With both the foibles of democracy and the perils of all-out war weighing ever more heavily on him as he grew older, Kennan became increasingly skeptical about the use of force as an instrument of American foreign policy.

Even if force could be wielded with great precision, it could not begin to accomplish most of the objectives of the United States in world affairs. At its best it was still too crude and bludgeoning an influence on peoples and events:

> We may defeat an enemy, but life goes on. The demands and aspirations of people, the compulsions that worked on them before they were defeated, begin to operate again after the defeat, unless you can do something to remove them. No victory can really be complete unless you eradicate the people against whom you were fighting or change basically the whole compulsions under which they live.[22]

Seven years later, Kennan rephrased the thought in one of his many pastoral images of international life:

> If there is any great lesson we Americans need to learn with regard to the methodology of foreign policy, it is that we must be gardeners and not mechanics in our approach to world affairs. We must come to think of the development of international life as an organic and not a mechanical process. We must realize that we did not create the forces by which this process operates. We must learn to take these forces for what they are, and to induce them to work with us and for us by influencing the environmental stimuli to which they are subjected, but to do this gently and patiently, with understanding and sympathy, not trying to force growth by mechanical means, not tearing the plants up by the roots when they fail to behave as we wish them to. The forces of nature

---

[22]NWC lecture, "What is Policy?" December 12, 1947, *Kennan Papers,* Box 17.

will generally be on the side of him who understands them best and respects them most scrupulously.[23]

The garden image may be a bit misleading, since Kennan does not mean to suggest that the process of international affairs is always pleasant or gentle. It should be kept in mind, perhaps, that gardening sometimes calls for the use of spades and hoes and pesticides, as well as earth and water and sun. "[T]here is a certain dialectic," Kennan wrote in the same volume, "involved in this question of influencing the attitudes and behavior of other peoples: a dialectic which means that the process is never fully effective unless people feel not only that our *favor* is a real possibility, attended by certain visible advantages to themselves, but that our *disfavor* would be, in certain circumstances, also a real possibility and would be attended by certain disadvantages to them." American policy, that is, must sometimes embrace "the harsh as well as the mild elements."[24]

For the most systematic treatment of this issue, as of most others, I must turn to Kennan's War College lectures. The very first of these lectures had set forth what, in Kennan's view, was the whole range of foreign policy instruments. It therefore merits brief summation here.[25]

International conflicts of interest, Kennan told his audience, traditionally had been settled in one of two broad ways: "adjustment" and "pressure." Kennan wished to see "adjustment"—good offices, mediation and conciliation, and international commissions of inquiry—used to every practical advantage, and these measures, applied by professional diplomats, would always be Kennan's preferred first approach to serving the national interest. But it was clear that "adjustment" alone could not settle basic disputes—and. it seemed particularly ill-suited to relations with the Soviet

---

[23]Kennan, *Realities of American Foreign Policy*, p. 93.
[24]Ibid., pp. 57–58 [emphasis in original].
[25]NWC lecture, "Measures Short of War (Diplomatic)," September 16, 1946, *Kennan Papers*, Box 16.

Union, which at the time explicitly rejected the possibility of a community of interest with capitalist nations. At least some of the time, then, the United States would have to apply "pressure."

There is pressure and there is pressure, and Kennan did not believe all forms were equally suitable to a democracy. Only a nation that was both centrally disciplined and essentially amoral in its foreign policy could employ the whole "repertoire" of pressure:

> The varieties of skulduggery which make up the repertoire of the totalitarian government are just about as unlimited as human ingenuity itself, and just about as unpleasant. For as you know, no holds are barred. There are no rules of the game. . . . [Totalitarian policy instruments] include persuasion, intimidation, deceit, corruption, penetration, subversion, horse-trading, bluffing, psychological pressure, economic pressure, seduction, blackmail, theft, fraud, rape, battle, murder and sudden death.

America's instruments of pressure, for reasons of temperament, aesthetics, or morality—Kennan did not say—were considerably more limited.

Kennan saw three broad categories of "measures short of war." The first was psychological. At their most direct, psychological measures included "informational activity like propaganda, or radio broadcast or distribution of magazines. . . ." Kennan would show, throughout his life, a writer's respect for the power of words and the importance of propaganda. In September of 1952, during his brief term as ambassador in Moscow, Kennan cabled Washington: "If we really mean business about diplomatic relations with them, then I should be down there in the Soviet Foreign Office three or four times a week complaining violently, loudly and publicly about the things they say, proving these things are false, getting publicity for my complaints and proofs. . . ."[26] In his BBC lectures five years later, he called it a "serious error to dismiss Soviet falsehoods as 'just propaganda'" and argued that propaganda is "a serious and important force in world affairs": "Let us not forget that these fantastic allegations are partially believed by those who say them, and they will be at least partially believed by many of those who listen. . . . Truth does not win over error just on its merits. It, too, has to be assiduously propagated."[27] But psychological measures, as Kennan meant them in his 1946 lecture, were also much broader and more indirect. "[O]ur government has begun to appreciate the fact," he said, "that anything it does of any importance at all has a psychological effect abroad as well as at home." Attitudes, to Kennan's mind, were the stuff of international politics, and to influence them was essential.[28]

The second category of "measures short of war" was economic. These measures included the granting or withholding of aid, the shrinking or expansion of trade, and economic pressures up to and including embargo.

The third category was "strictly political measures," involving alliances and world opinion. Its chief means was "the cultivation of solidarity with other like minded nations on every given issue of our foreign policy." Finally, there was a general rule of *quid pro quo*: "I would like to see our government take over the maximum amount of control of all the facilities in this country which can benefit foreign states. And in the case of those foreign states which we must regard as rivals to our power, I would like to see us turn these controls on and off like a faucet, exactly in proportion to the treatment we ourselves get abroad."

---

[26]Quoted in *Memoirs* II, p. 160.

[27]Kennan, *Russia, the Atom and the West*, pp. 29–30.

[28]See also, *American Diplomacy*, p. 11, in which Kennan identifies "such things as fear, ambition, insecurity, jealousy, and perhaps even boredom" as "prime movers of events."

III

Kennan's views on the relationship between these nonmilitary instruments and the maintenance and employment of armed force are complicated and somewhat hard to pin down. As might be expected of a man who was reading Clausewitz and Machiavelli and working with Bernard Brodie at the War College, Kennan devoted considerable thought to this relationship.

At first, in the immediate postwar period, Kennan tended to stress—as did the classical strategists before him—the continuity between war and politics, force and pressure, military and nonmilitary instruments of policy. Even in the first War College lecture, Kennan premised his discussion of "measures short of war" on "a preponderance of [American] strength in the world" and a "readiness to use it at any time if we are pushed beyond certain limits." It should surprise no one to be told that Kennan did not define those limits, but he did say what he did *not* mean: force should not be used for "blustering, threatening, waving clubs at people and telling them if they don't do this or that we are going to drop a bomb on them." Still, military power would have to be incorporated into a peacetime strategy: "[W]e must cease to have separate patterns of measures— one pattern for peace and one pattern for war. We must rather select them according to the purposes we are pursuing and classify them that way."[29]

Often expressed in the next decade, with slowly diminishing enthusiasm, was the idea that military power— even where not actually used—had political repercussions and rendered other instruments of the national will more potent. "You have no idea," Kennan said in 1946, "how much it contributes to the general politeness and pleasantness of diplomacy when you have a little quiet armed force in

---

[29]NWC lecture, "Measures Short of War (Diplomatic)," *Kennan Papers*, Box 16.

the background. People who otherwise are very insulting and very violent become just as pleasant:—why, they couldn't be nicer if they belonged to the same golf club and played golf together every Sunday morning."[30] For this reason, Kennan wrote two years later, a strong and alert military force "is probably the most important single instrumentality in the conduct of U.S. foreign policy."[31]

It was implicit, in fact, in much that Kennan would say about "power realities" in years to come,[32] that military power had political penumbras. To take just one example, Kennan recounted at least twice how the Allies' need for Russian help in World War II meant that the military victory was "mortgaged in advance" and that "there would be a heavy political charge" against it.[33] Military power, moreover, did not have to be used to make it politically effective. "Armaments," he said in 1957, "are important not just for what could be done with them in time of war, but for the psychological shadows they cast in time of peace." This only echoed the closing words of a lecture ten years before: "[T]he towers of the Kremlin cast a long shadow. . . . And that, gentlemen, is a dangerous thing; for the more I see of the life of this international society the more I am convinced that it is the shadows rather than the substance of things that move the hearts, and sway the deeds, of statesmen."[34]

In more recent years, Kennan's emphasis has shifted radically in response to what he sees as an overmilitarized view of the tools of American power. One critic now finds it possible to assert, ludicrously, that "Kennan has never accepted the Roman maxim, 'Si vis pacem, pare bellum.'"[35]

---

[30]Ibid.

[31]Private paper, "Comments on the General Trend of U.S. Foreign Policy," *Kennan Papers*, Box 23.

[32]See Chapter 2.

[33]Kennan, *American Diplomacy*, p. 68. See also *Russia and the West*, p. 361.

[34]Kennan, *Russia, the Atom and the West*, p. 93; NWC lecture, "Planning of Foreign Policy," June 18, 1947, *Kennan Papers*, Box 17.

[35]Rostow, "Searching for Kennan's Grand Design."

Actually, as recounted above, Kennan has always both counseled preparedness and warned against the danger of regarding American power in purely military terms. But it is true that since the mid-1960s he has also tried to downplay the political significance of armed force. A "momentary superiority in weaponry," he wrote in 1964, does not permit one state to force political terms on another. In 1977—less unexceptionably—he went a long step further: "The belief that stronger powers dominate weaker ones and dictate terms to them simply by the possession of superior military force, or by demands placed under the threat of the use of such force, has extremely slender support in historical experience."[36] With a bit of gymnastics, Kennan could probably reconcile this last statement with the ones he made in the 1940s and 1950s on the same subject, but he would at least have to concede that his stress has changed.

Exactly how and why it has changed is not easy to discover with any precision. It seems to be, in part, simply another example of Kennan's tendency to see himself as counterweight to the seesaw of official opinion. At least since his Moscow ambassadorship, Kennan has believed that, just as there is a continuity and interdependence between military power and political objects, there is also "an incurable conflict in certain respects" between them. The conflict, he said in 1952, takes two forms. First, an over-emphasis on military power "would be quite disruptive of the political resistance of the Western peoples." Second, attempting to build armaments to ideal levels in terms of their usefulness in case of a war with the Soviet Union would also make war more likely. "The requirements of either of these approaches, the military or the political," Kennan wrote, "would—if carried to extremes—be quite destructive

---

[36]Kennan, *On Dealing with the Communist World*, pp. 14–15; *The Cloud of Danger*, p. 124.

of the requirements of the other."[37] Kennan saw Washington as moving toward the military extreme, and so he began reacting against it.

That reaction led him, finally, to an apparent rule of thumb that the United States should use military force only to defend its "vital interests."[38] Viewed historically, as Kennan's once-colleague Bernard Brodie points out, this is almost tautology: nations have always justified the use of force with an assertion that the interests at stake were "vital" to them.[39] Kennan's novelty is that he seems to believe he can more or less precisely delimit vital from nonvital interests in advance, and therefore that he can define those interests which are worth defending with force and those which are not. I argued in Chapter 2 that this is a strategic fallacy, though it may well be useful if it is not considered a rigid guide to action. In any case, Kennan is more or less aware of the theoretical difficulties. He is simply more concerned with the alternative danger of overmilitarized thinking.

The general conclusion that may be drawn with regard to Kennan's philosophy of politics and war—at least until the late 1970s—is that he saw armed force as essential, as much for its political as its military value, and he urged considerable circumspection about its actual use. That does not mean he never thought of using force. It has been pointed out

---

[37]Kennan, "The Soviet Union and the Atlantic Pact," telegraphic message of September 8, 1952, reprinted in *Memoirs* II, pp. 349–51. See also, for discussions of capabilities versus intentions and the political–military tradeoff: *Realities of American Foreign Policy*, pp. 69–70, 82–83; *Russia and the West*, pp. 330, 379; *Memoirs* I, pp. 395, 475; *Memoirs* II, pp. 38, 140, 141, 336; *The Cloud of Danger*, pp. 210–11.

[38]This is never stated explicitly, but it seems the only possible conclusion from Kennan's discussion of "vital" and "serious" interests and military force in *The Cloud of Danger*, pp. 80–81.

[39]Bernard Brodie, *War & Politics* (New York: MacMillan Publishing Co., Inc., 1973), p. 2.

more than once[40] that Kennan is on record as having considered the possibility of military intervention in Greece in 1947, in Italy in 1948, and on Taiwan in 1949. What is less often mentioned is that Kennan never actually *recommended* such intervention.[41] He did, of course, support the use of American troops in Korea in 1950. And in 1980, in surprisingly little-remarked testimony before the Senate Foreign Relations Committee, Kennan advocated a declaration of war against Iran over the hostage issue. This advice was geared more to the legal than the military relationship, but Kennan also urged that the United States "hold in readiness" military strikes against the Khomeini government.[42]

IV

So: what of containment? The X-Article was widely seen as a prescription for military "counter-force" around the globe, and yet Kennan himself now says his idea was "not the containment by military means of a military threat, but the political containment of a political threat."[43] The seeming turnabout has variously bemused and enraged Kennan's critics. One says that Kennan's views, considered as dialectical exercises, contain thesis and antithesis—but no synthesis. Another thinks it "odd that the father of containment now yearns to be author of its abandonment—as if Einstein, on second thought, had repudiated the ominous $E = mc^2$, thus

---

[40]Wright, "Mr. 'X' and Containment," p. 29; Mark, "The Question of Containment," p. 435; Gaddis, *Strategies of Containment*, p. 39n.

[41]See *FR:1947*, V, pp. 468–69; *FR:1948*, III, pp. 848–49; *FR:1949*, IX, pp. 356–69. Only Gaddis (p. 39n) makes clear that Kennan did not in the end come down positively for intervention.

[42]Don Oberdorfer, "George Kennan Urges Tougher Stand on Iran," *The Washington Post*, February 28, 1980. Kennan reaffirmed this position in an interview nearly a year later. See *The Washington Post*, January 4, 1981.

[43]Kennan, *Memoirs* I, p. 358.

to shed his Nobel Prize in physics for the nobler peace prize." Still another, noting that Kennan often claims to be misunderstood, is distinctly unsympathetic ("What rotten luck!") and inclined to believe that Kennan

> produces arguments straight from the French *Fable de la Chauve-Souris* (The Bat's Fable).
> He either says:

>> *Je suis oiseau; voyez mes ailes;*
>> *Vive la gens qui fend les aires!*

>> [I am a bird; look at my wings;
>> Long live those who take to the winds!]

> Or, if necessary, he retorts:

>> *Je suis souris; vivant les rats;*
>> *Jupiter confonds les chats!*

>> [I am a mouse; long live rats;
>> Jupiter confound the cats!][44]

It is surely uncharitable, and wrong besides, to assume that Kennan's admitted dual nature reflects some opportunistic taint. Perhaps it is more nearly correct to state that Kennan really *is* part bird and part mouse.

Earlier in this book I said that the broad strategy of containment had three ends: to restore a balance of power and build up war-stricken allies, to exploit tensions in the then-monolithic Communist International and thereby to reduce Moscow's means of projecting power, and (in the long run) to moderate and negotiate Soviet global behavior.[45] In light of those ends and of Kennan's view of the instruments of foreign policy, it should be abundantly clear that to brand containment simply a "military" or a "political" doctrine is—I'll quote Einstein here since he

---

[44]Rostow, "Searching for Kennan's Grand Design"; Seabury, "George Kennan versus Mr. 'X'," p. 17; Leopold Labedz, "A Last Critique," in *Encounters with Kennan*, pp. 169–70.

[45]See Chapter 2, pp. 46–47.

seems to have been brought into the argument—to make everything not only "as simple as possible," but "more so."

Only one of the three fundamental objectives of containment, that of the gradual "mellowing" of Soviet power, could even conceivably be achieved by military means alone. None of them could be achieved without any military power whatever. The labels "military" and "political" are therefore not very helpful in describing Kennan's tactical plans. Still, it seems clear that Kennan did not think armed force was to be the primary instrument even of reforming Soviet power. If I had to pick a label, then, "political" would seem closer to the truth. And so I arrive at the question: what did Kennan mean by "counter-force"?[46]

Kennan now says he regrets the "careless and indiscriminate language of the X-Article," and he points particularly to the use of "counter-force" as an example.[47] Curiously, though, he cites little evidence from his early writings to bolster the claim that more careful drafting would have averted the misleading impression of counter-force as an essentially military concept. But very good evidence on this point is available in the Kennan Papers. That evidence is of two sorts, which I will call semantic "omission" and "commission" for the sake of convenience.

The first sort, some of which has been published by John Lewis Gaddis, rests on the observation that in all Kennan's writings apart from the X-Article one would be hard pressed to find a single use of "counter-force" in prescriptive terms. This is, in other words, an argument from omission. The term Kennan does use—often—is "counterpressure." I will return to this distinction below.[48]

---

[46]The context, again, was: "Soviet pressure against the free institutions of the western world is something that can be contained by the adroit and vigilant application of counter-force at a series of constantly shifting geographical and political points. . . . " See [Kennan], "The Sources of Soviet Conduct," p. 576.

[47]Kennan, *Memoirs* I, pp. 359–60.

[48]See Gaddis, *Strategies of Containment*, pp. 48–51; "Containment: A Reassessment," pp. 877–78.

The second sort of evidence is more positive: at least once in 1947, Kennan crossed out the word "pressure" and inserted "force" in a discussion of how *not* to achieve a change in the nature of Soviet power. The passage, in draft form, read as follows:

> The shape of Soviet power is like that of a tree which has been bent in its infancy and twisted into a certain pattern. It can be gradually caused to grow back into another form; but not by any sudden or violent application of *pressure*. This effect can be produced only by the exertion of steady *pressure* over a period of years in the right direction.[49]

Corrections made in Kennan's hand changed the passage significantly:

> The shape of Soviet power is like that of a tree which has been bent in its infancy and twisted into a certain pattern. It can be caused to grow back into another form; but not by any sudden or violent application of *force*. This effect can be produced only by the exertion of steady *pressure* over a period of years in the right direction.[50]

This editing change is extremely suggestive, to say the least. Kennan altered the passage deliberately to emphasize a contrast between force and pressure. And pressure, it will be recalled, is Kennan's term for a whole range of foreign policy instruments, including political, psychological, and economic "measures short of war."

The tools of containment, in other words, like the tools of American foreign policy in general, were many. True, Kennan did not see much prospect for "adjustment" of difficulties with the Kremlin. In a lecture given only one day after he outlined the instruments of American power at the

---

[49]"Russian–American Relations," draft lecture prepared for delivery at the University of Virginia, February 20, 1947, *Kennan Papers*, Box 16 [emphasis added].

[50]Ibid.; note also that Kennan deleted the word "gradually."

War College, Kennan emphasized that the United States could not influence Soviet leaders

> by reasoning with them, by arguing with them, by going to them and saying: "Look here, this is the way things are." I don't believe that is possible. . . . I think we should go to them and put it right on the line, but not with the idea that they are going to turn around and say: "By George, I never thought of that before. We will go right back and change our policies." . . . They aren't that kind of people.

But neither could force accomplish all—nor most—of what Kennan hoped to manage. America could change Soviet attitudes and behavior only

> by the logic of a long-term set of circumstances which makes it evident that noncollaborative purposes on their part will not pay—will redound to Russia's disadvantage, whereas a more kindly policy toward us would win them advantages. If we can keep them maneuvered into a position where it is always hard and unprofitable for them to take action contrary to the principles of the United Nations and to our policies and where there is always an open door and an easy road to collaboration . . . I personally am quite convinced . . . that sooner or later the logic of it will penetrate their government and will force changes there.

Kennan went on to argue, just as he would argue in the X-Article, that the Soviets did not want an immediate showdown with the United States. That fact, Kennan said, "should enable us, if our policies are wise and nonprovocative, to contain them both militarily and politically for a long time to come."[51]

---

[51]Stenographic transcript, Lecture to Foreign Service and Department Personnel, September 17, 1946, *Kennan Papers*, Box 16. Kennan points out in his *Memoirs* I, p. 304, that this—not the X-Article—was his first use of the verb "contain" in reference to the Soviet Union.

Kennan elaborated in a War College lecture late in 1947. To create counterpressure, he said, "you marshall all the forces at your disposal on the world chessboard" to contain the Soviets. "I mean not only the military forces you have," he added, "although that is very important, but all the political forces. You just have to dispose of your pawns, your queens and kings in such a way that the Russian sees it is going to be in his interest to do what you want him to do. . . ."[52] Kennan summed up in what Gaddis calls (with the apparent support of Kennan's *Memoirs, 1925–1950*) "a preliminary version of the 'X' article": "The problem of meeting the Kremlin in international affairs therefore boils down to this: Its inherent expansive tendencies must be firmly contained at all times by counterpressure which makes it constantly evident that attempts to break through this containment would be detrimental to *Soviet* interests."[53]

Kennan's use of the term "expansive tendencies" in the X-Article and its early drafts was not meant to suggest the military expansion of Soviet territorial bounds:

> The Russians don't want to invade anyone. It is not in their tradition. They tried it once in Finland and got their fingers burned. They don't want war of any kind. Above all, they don't want the open responsibility that

---

[52]NWC lecture, "Soviet Diplomacy," October 6, 1947, *Kennan Papers*, Box 17.

[53]Private paper, "The Soviet Way of Thought and Its Effect on Foreign Policy," January 24, 1947, *Kennan Papers*, Box 16 [emphasis in original]. Kennan delivered an identically titled lecture to the Council on Foreign Relations in New York on January 7, and the paper he wrote for James Forrestal (later identified in print by Arthur Krock) was dated January 31. There is no record of either of these in the Kennan Papers, and so the January 24 paper is the closest surviving approximation of a "draft" of the X-Article. See Gaddis, "Containment: A Reassessment," p. 877; Kennan, *Memoirs* I, pp. 355–56.

See also Kennan's reference to the "manipulation of our political *and* military forces in such a way that the Russians will always be confronted with superior strength. . . . " ("Russia," Naval War College Lecture, October 1, 1946, *Kennan Papers*, Box 16).

open invasion brings with it. They far prefer to do the job politically with stooge forces. Note well: when I say politically, that does not mean without violence. But it means that the violence is nominally *domestic*, not *international* violence. It is, if you will, a police violence . . . not a military violence.

The policy of containment related to the effort to encourage other peoples to resist this type of violence and to defend the *internal* integrity of their countries.[54]

Eduard Mark cites this passage in arguing that Kennan's "political" containment actually "foreshadowed later military involvement throughout the world," because it would take military force to respond even to nominally political violence. C. Ben Wright, similarly, tries to make it look as if Kennan often—even consistently—thought of containment in terms of military force.[55] Both miss the point. Yes, Kennan did sometimes consider military intervention, and in one case—Korea—he actively recommended it. Yes, force was indeed one of the instruments of pressure in the "repertoire" of the United States. But Mark and Wright clearly generalize from slender evidence and largely ignore the bulk of what Kennan said and wrote about containment.

There is simply no way around the fact, manifest in Kennan's published and unpublished record, that he consistently downplayed the military aspect of containment and emphasized the political and psychological danger that war-weakened nations—especially in Western Europe—would fall victim to the "long shadow" of the Kremlin and allow Communist parties subservient to Moscow to take power. "Remember," he told a War College audience in 1947, "that . . . as things stand today, it is not Russian military power which is threatening us, it is Russian political power." A year later he urged that the planned NATO pact

---

[54]Unsent letter to Walter Lippmann, April 6, 1948, quoted in *Memoirs* I, pp. 361–62 [emphasis in original].

[55]Mark, "What Kind of Containment?" pp. 96, 99–100; Wright, "Mr. 'X' and Containment."

"not be regarded as the main answer to the Russian effort to achieve domination over Western Europe, nor as a replacement for other needed steps." In 1954 he called "hopes for the demoralization and disintegration of our world" the chief Soviet design, and he said that again in 1957. All in all, Kennan held to this view with remarkable consistency.[56]

This view of containment emphasized the nonmilitary instruments of American power—of which the Marshall Plan was a prime example. Containment was not even necessarily a question of relations with the Soviet Union:

> [T]he problem of containment is basically a problem of the reactions of people within the non-communist world. It is true that this condition depends upon the maintenance by ourselves and our allies, at all times, of an adequate defense posture, designed to guard against misunderstandings and to give confidence and encouragement to the weak and the fainthearted. But so long as that posture is maintained, the things that need most to be done to prevent the further expansion of Soviet power are not, so far as we are concerned, things we can do directly in our relations with the Soviet government; they are things we must do in our relations with the peoples of the non-communist world.[57]

And this emphasis, especially after Europe's economic recovery, brought Kennan back to familiar themes: the force of the American example in world affairs, the "how" as opposed to the "what," and the notion of good form and national dignity.

Eventually, Kennan believed, the basis of Soviet–American competition would be the respective societies themselves—the inner core of vitality and resilience that preoccupied him before, during, and long after the time he

---

[56] NWC lecture, "What is Policy?" December 18, 1947, *Kennan Papers*, Box 17; "Considerations Affecting the Conclusion of a North Atlantic Treaty," November 23, 1948, quoted in *Memoirs* I, pp. 410–11; *Realities of American Foreign Policy*, p. 71; *Russia, the Atom and the West*, p. 91.

[57] Kennan, *Realities of American Foreign Policy*, p. 87.

wrote the X-Article. The competition would amount to "a sort of long-range fencing match in which the weapons are not only the development of military power but the loyalties and convictions of hundreds of millions of people and the control or influence over their forms of political organization. . . . It may be the strength and health of our respective systems which is decisive and which will determine the issue."[58] If Americans could pull themselves together, solve their own internal problems, show themselves to be on their way to curing the common ills of societies in the modern age, then they would have reason for optimism about the potential of American power in world affairs. If they could not, then it would not take an act of the Soviets to bring about their decline and final fall.

---

[58]"Current Problems of Soviet–American Relations," Naval Academy, Annapolis, May 9, 1947, *Kennan Papers*, Box 17.

SIX

On the Decline
of the West

> It is usually when one is about to despair of Americans that they suddenly show their greatest qualities.
>
> *Kennan, 1957*

> I grew up with a certain faith in American civilization and a certain belief that the American experiment was a positive development in the history of mankind. . . . I [now] think this country is destined to succumb to failures which cannot be other than tragic and enormous in their scope. All this, of course, is not an easy thing to live with.
>
> *Kennan, 1975*

It is hard to read any large chunk of Kennan's writings in a compressed period of time without taking note of their basic interconnections. Kennan's life work has about it something of the tenor of a complicated fugue: rhythmically irregular, apparently all but random in its organization—but woven, almost despite itself, into a tightly braided whole. Motifs appear and fade, only to reappear, elaborated, and then fade again in bewildering succession. Sometimes it can be as infuriating as bewildering, because the fugue, taken a few bars at a time, seems to make no structural sense. It is perhaps this quality of Kennan's writing that accounts for the generally, though not universally, poor quality of its critics' response and the almost comical misunderstandings on which much of that response has been based. Still, beneath all the digressions, there is a unifying theme. Kennan always returns to it eventually. And so that theme, stripped of its counterpoint, must be the subject of this sixth and final chapter.

That theme is this: the quality of a civilization is the only true measure of its purposes, its methods, and its prospects in world affairs. A society's internal health is logically precedent to its relationship with the external world. The role of American power in international life cannot be sensibly discussed until its role at home is clear.

Kennan prides himself in his detachment as an observer,[1] and when he looks at American life he does not like what he sees. His picture of the United States—sometimes, more broadly, "the West"—began with discomfort and warning and has descended with time into gloom and despair. It is this loss of faith in American society, more even than his loss of faith in democracy, that has marked the progression of his views on the more traditional questions of foreign affairs.

---

[1]"None of us," he wrote in *Memoirs* I, p. 8, "has all the qualities to be a good observer of his age; I am conscious of being lacking in a number of them; but it helps in this respect, however lonely and unsettling it may be in others, to be the guest of one's time and not a member of its household." See also p. 77.

I

From at least the late 1930s, Kennan has "never ceased to ponder . . . the obvious deterioration in the quality both of American life and of the natural environment in which it had its being, under the impact of a headlong overpopulation, industrialization, commercialization and urbanization of society."[2] Add to these four phenomena the less tangible qualities of "internal disharmony, dissension, intolerance and the things that break up the real moral and political structure of our society at home,"[3] and you have a *précis* of Kennan's State of the Union.

Oddly, though Kennan's whole philosophy of foreign affairs is derivative of his domestic views, he has always been somehow self-conscious when addressing himself to the weaknesses of American society. "I have tried not to speak much about domestic affairs," he wrote in 1968, "because I have not really had time to study them and there are so many people who know more about them than I do." He added: "I have had other things to do in life. Not everyone can do everything."[4] As a result, his writings on this subject most often take the form of parentheses and long asides.

A preponderance of Kennan's concern turns on "what the machine does to man,"[5] or the impact of technology on society. He does not get four sentences into his memoirs before referring to "the ruthless destruction of setting which the explosions of . . . technological change have so often worked."[6] By 1975, Kennan had come up with what he called a "major conclusion":

---

[2]Kennan, *Memoirs* II, p. 85.
[3]NWC lecture, September 16, 1946, *Kennan Papers*, Box 16.
[4]Kennan, *Democracy and the Student Left*, pp. 227–28, 236.
[5]Kennan, *Russia, the Atom and the West*, p. 110.
[6]Kennan, *Memoirs* I, p. 3.

[T]he older I get, and the more I occupy myself with the history of the past century in Europe and the United States, the more I am persuaded that the Industrial Revolution itself was the source of most of the bewilderments and failures of the modern age. This does not, of course, mean to say that there should have been no technological improvements in the early 19th century; but it does mean that the revolution in technology should never have been allowed to go uncontrolled as it did, that one should have examined each improvement in technology very carefully with a view to its total impact on society. . . . I can't see the answer to the problems of modern civilization of our highly urbanized industrial society. This society bears the seeds of its own horrors—unbreathable air, undrinkable water, starvation—and until people realize that we have to get back to a much simpler form of life, a much smaller population, a society in which the agrarian component is far greater again in relation to the urban component . . . I can see no answer to the troubles of our time.[7]

Industrial changes, conceived as the scientific path to progress, are rather "an appalling regression."[8]

"Control," in turn, recurs often in Kennan's discussions of technological change. The "precipitous and uncontrolled" workings of modernization have led to the "partial disintegration of many of our large urban communities, the general deterioration of social environment in large portions of those communities, and the chaotic and often unsatisfactory manner in which new communities are being permitted to come into existence." Because of this, Kennan said in 1954, "others" around the world "feel that we are not really the masters of our own fate, that our society is not really under control, that we are being helplessly carried along by forces we do not have the courage or the vitality to master."[9]

---

[7]Kennan and Urban, "A Conversation," p. 4.
[8]Ibid., p. 6.
[9]Kennan, *Realities of American Foreign Policy*, pp. 112–14.

Even in 1954, Kennan identified himself with those "others." It was all but inconceivable to him that Americans could so enshrine uninhibited self-interest and *laissez faire* that they exerted no control whatever over the diffusion of technology into society. "Such things as the automobile, the telephone, radio, and television were not planned or deliberately selected for their social implications," he wrote. " . . . If someone were to come along tomorrow, as perhaps someone will, with another invention no less devastating than these others in its effects on our personal lives, we would submit to it without a murmur."[10] He did not, in 1954, attack this state of affairs directly, but he scarcely hid his amazement. Five years later, he had made up his mind:

> Let science, by all means, be free. But its application to human life must be the object of man's sharpest distrust, and of the most severe social discipline. All of this points . . . to more *"dirigisme,"* not less, in Western society. I am sorry about this. To my mind, it is unfortunate. But I can see no escape from it.[11]

E. H. Carr once wrote that he had never heard "of a historian who said that, in view of the cost, it would have been better to stay the hand of progress and not industrialize; if any such exists, he belongs to the school of Chesterton and Belloc, and will—quite properly—not be taken seriously by serious historians."[12] Kennan does not go quite so far as to regret industrialization altogether, but he clearly wishes—and seems to think it possible—to slow, and even reverse, its pace.

Of all the gadgets and mechanical afflictions of modern man, the automobile is the worst. It is "surely the most wasteful, antisocial, and environmentally pernicious means

---

[10]Ibid., p. 10.

[11]George F. Kennan and Melvin J. Lasky, "A Conversation," in *Encounters with Kennan*, p. 214.

[12]E. H. Carr, *What Is History?* (New York: Vintage Books, 1961), p. 104.

of moving human bodies about that has ever been devised."[13] It is "a dirty, noisy . . . and lonely means of travel," which

> pollutes the air, ruins the safety and sociability of the street, and exercises upon the individual a discipline which takes away far more freedom than it gives him. It causes an enormous amount of land to be unnecessarily abstracted from nature and from plant life and to become devoid of any natural function. It explodes cities, grievously impairs the whole institution of neighborliness, fragmentizes and destroys communities.[14]

"And what disturbs me most," Kennan writes, "is not only that these mechanical legs have a deleterious effect on man himself, drugging him into a sort of paralysis. . . . What disturbs me most is his abject dependence on this means of transportation and on the complicated processes that make it possible."[15]

Related to, perhaps even superseding, the question of what the machine does to man is the question of what man—with his machines—does to nature. "[N]o longer," Kennan said as early as 1954, "[can we] permit the economic advance of our country to take place so extensively at the cost of the devastation of its natural resources and its natural beauty."[16] This is a question, he added in 1968,

> not just of our own once so magnificent continent, which we are treating with the blind destructiveness of the army ant; it is a question of the purity and life-sustaining quality of the seas and the global atmosphere within which this continent, and we with it, has its existence. How long can man go on overpopulating this planet, destroying its topsoils, slashing off its forests, exhausting its supplies of fresh water, tearing

---

[13]Kennan, *The Cloud of Danger*, p. 20.
[14]Kennan, *Democracy and the Student Left*, p. 232.
[15]Diary, November 4, 1951, quoted in *Memoirs* II, p. 81.
[16]Kennan, *Realities of American Foreign Policy*, p. 111.

away at its mineral resources, consuming its oxygen with a wild proliferation of machines, making sewers of its rivers and seas, producing industrial poisons of the most deadly sort and distributing them liberally into its atmosphere, its streams and its ocean beds, disregarding and destroying the ecology of its plant and insect life? Not much longer, I suspect. I may not witness the beginning of the disaster on a serious scale. But many of [today's students] will.[17]

In 1970 he was moved to write a journal article, starkly titled "To Prevent a World Wasteland."[18] And by 1977, his urgency yet more apparent, he wrote that "the strains this problem is going to impose on our society in the coming years are going to be severe beyond anything heretofore contemplated."[19]

Ranking only just behind environmental destruction, for Kennan, is the "debauching" phenomenon of American advertising, and in particular the "extent to which it has been permitted to dominate and exploit the entire process of public communication in our country."

It is to me positively inconceivable that the whole great, infinitely responsible function of mass communication, including very important phases of the educational process, should be farmed out—as something to be mined for whatever profit there may be in it—to people whose function and responsibility have nothing to do with the truth—whose function and responsibility, in fact, are concerned with the peddling of what is, by definition, untruth. . . . After the heedless destruction of natural environment, I regard this . . . as probably the greatest evil of our national life.[20]

What exactly Kennan means to say here is a bit of a mystery.

---

[17]Kennan, *Democracy and the Student Left*, p. 229.
[18]George F. Kennan, "To Prevent a World Wasteland: A Proposal," *Foreign Affairs*, April 1970, pp. 401–13.
[19]Kennan, *The Cloud of Danger*, p. 24.
[20]Kennan, *Democracy and the Student Left*, p. 231.

His target, he writes, is "not advertising as such, but the consignment to the advertiser of the entire mass communications process." But he also says this consignment "pollutes the entire content of information that flows back and forth in the country" and that it "de-trains people for any sustained attention to the truth."[21]

If it is not "advertising as such" that Kennan condemns, then he must believe that advertisements poison the editorial content of newspapers, magazines, and broadcast media. This, it seems to me, is a rather unpromising argument to attempt. It either confuses advertisers with publishers, or it argues deliberately that the one is effectively the other—which it is difficult plausibly to do. Yet Kennan does seem to urge this conclusion:

> Is it a revolution I am demanding? Yes—a revolution in the financing and control of the process of communication generally. And if this revolution brings in the government as a replacement for the advertiser in many of these processes, I still wish for it. The government's commitment and conscience as an educator—its commitment to truthfulness and integrity in communication—may not be all that we could want. But it has at least *some* responsibility here to the public weal, and *some* obligation to keep in mind the public needs. This is more than one can say about the advertiser.[22]

It is astonishing to me that Kennan can so blithely, in all of two paragraphs, discard the bulk of the Anglo–American tradition of an independent, privately financed press, and with so little concept of a proper replacement. The government ("if" the revolution leads to this) might not be so bad a publisher, Kennan figures, though he seems to have thought somewhat less highly of its commitment to truthfulness and integrity at the height of Senator McCarthy's sway,[23] and

---

[21]Ibid., and Kennan and Urban, "A Conversation," p. 16.

[22]Kennan, *Democracy and the Student Left*, p. 232 [emphasis in original].

[23]Kennan, *Memoirs* II, pp. 190–228.

later, during the Watergate affair. I can account for Kennan's irresponsibility on this subject only in two ways. First, there is his yearning, as detailed in prevous chapters, for objective truth, and his habit of attributing differences of opinion to failures of understanding. There is little room in this conception for the Millian view of the truth as an ideal that is best approached by the clash of opinions—however misguided, silly, pernicious, or sophistical many of them may be. Kennan, of course, is entitled to disagree with this concept if he likes, but he should at least say why. Second, there is—as in some of his discussions of democracy—an undiscriminating frustration. *The New York Times*, he once wrote, only half in jest, is "committed to a policy . . . of publishing anything trivial that I might have to say and ignoring everything of importance."[24] As for lesser organs of communication, they are callow, shallow, full of slogans and half-truths. *Something* obviously needs to be done, and perhaps Kennan feels justified in demanding a revolution without exerting himself overmuch to plan it. If so, he becomes uncomfortably like the "Rebels without a Program" he derides.[25]

Most of Kennan's concerns about American society, of course, are a great deal less exceptionable: the disintegration of cities, the appalling dimensions of violent crime, inflation, unemployment, poor public transportation, decaying educational standards, and decadence in general. These are most often expressed as lists, and it is better to quote Kennan directly on these than to summarize, for in summary is lost some of the cumulative quality of his distress. "What is at stake here," he wrote to a correspondent in 1952,

> is our duty to ourselves and our own national ideals. When individual citizens no longer find themselves unhappy in our country merely by virtue of their race or

---

[24]Ibid., p. 173.
[25]Kennan, *Democracy and the Student Left*, pp. 1–20.

color; when our cities no longer reek with graft and corruption; when criminal elements are no longer close to the source of local power in many of our larger urban communities; when we have cleared away our slums and filth and blighted areas; when we have taken in hand the question of juvenile delinquency . . . ; when we have revived the meaning of community and citizenship for the urban dweller in general; when we have overcome inflation; when we have had the courage to recognize the educational effect of our mass media as a public responsibility and to find for them the place they should properly have in a healthy and progressive society; . . . when we have taken real measures . . . to protect the beauty and healthfulness of the land God gave us to live on and to restore in general a harmonious and stable relationship between the American man and his incomparable natural environment—when we have done such things, then, in my opinion, we shall have achieved spiritual distinction . . . and the world will be well aware of that achievement.[26]

When we have done such things, Kennan might have added, we will have done what no civilization elsewhere—or before us, or, likely, to come—has ever done: solved all our major problems.

II

Here, then, is Kennan's America: selfish, vulgar, mechanized beyond nature's recognition, materialistic, undisciplined . . . and getting worse.

Or, at least, Kennan's view of it is getting worse. A chronological tour through his writings on the prospects of

---

[26]Quoted in Kennan, *Memoirs* II, pp. 84–85. There is a similar—even longer—list in *Russia, the Atom and the West*, pp. 110–11. The list on pp. 19–26 of *The Cloud of Danger* is also much the same in content but far and away bleaker in tone.

Western society is profoundly depressing—not only because it details the painful loss of faith by one man, but because that man makes so powerful an indictment of his society.

The diseases Kennan describes, under the omnibus label of "decline," have always had a place in his writings, but the prognosis has changed rather radically over the years. In 1954, for instance, he said this:

> If I did not believe that, despite all our national failings, our existence as a great nation was by and large beneficial to the civilization of which we are a part, if I did not believe that our purposes as a nation were on balance worthy ones . . . I would not feel we were entitled to take the attitude I have suggested this evening. As it is, I do.[27]

The X-Article, seven years earlier, had maintained that America "need only measure up to its own best traditions" to avoid destruction.[28] And however much he deplored this or that aspect of American society in the 1930s, 1940s, and 1950s, Kennan kept the faith. If he did not flatly affirm that the United States *would* solve its problems and help create a better world, he said at least, "I can only say that I don't see why not."[29]

Why not? Kennan seemed to repeat the question, as much to himself as to the reading public, all through the 1950s. "It is usually when one is about to despair of Americans that they suddenly show their greatest qualities," Kennan wrote in the seventh (never delivered) Reith lecture of 1957. He *was* about to despair, and he waited with eroding patience for those great qualities to emerge: "Personally, I do not believe in this thesis of decadence: I think there are still great sources of strength in both peoples [American and British], of which we ourselves are poorly conscious and

---

[27]Kennan, *Realities of American Foreign Policy*, pp. 61–62.
[28][Kennan], "The Sources of Soviet Conduct," p. 582.
[29]"Russia," Naval War College lecture, October 1, 1946, *Kennan Papers*, Box 16.

about which the non-European world knows nothing." Here is how he closed the last delivered Reith lecture:

> In the conclusion of the X-Article, to which I referred at the outset of these talks, I cited a passage from the American writer Thoreau. Today, under the shadow of the hydrogen bomb and of all the materialism and faintheartedness of our time, I am going to recall this passage to mind once more. . . . "There is no ill," Thoreau wrote, "which may not be dissipated, like the dark, if you let in a stronger light upon it. . . . If the light we use is but a paltry and narrow taper, most objects will cast a shadow wider than themselves."[30]

Kennan's own criticisms, which he aired with increasing passion, were meant to be part of the "stronger light" that would dissipate the West's ills by exposing them. In a revealing interview with Melvin Lasky in 1959, Kennan reeled off much the same list of problems as he would today, but in a much more constructive tone.[31] He explicitly deplored, in fact, an unrestrained pessimism: "I have been rather disappointed in our own American literature. We have had a whole series of novels which gave a bitterly critical picture of society, but so many of these books appear to me to reflect in their cynicism and in their hopelessness precisely the same evils against which they were written." When Lasky likened America to a cancer patient, Kennan replied: "The analogy you offer is faulty, because one cannot regard American society as hopelessly diseased. Every bit of self-scrutiny in a democratic society is healthy, and as our society is going to go on, for better or for worse, barring some catastrophe of the atom, it is certainly bound to be influenced by honest and penetrating self-criticism."[32]

---

[30]Kennan, *Russia, the Atom and the West*, pp. 99, 113, 114. Actually, Kennan did not quote Thoreau in the X-Article. He cited a somewhat similar passage from Thomas Mann's *Buddenbrooks*.

[31]Kennan and Lasky, "A Conversation," pp. 198–99.

[32]Ibid., pp. 195, 197.

This was close to the last of Kennan's optimism, or, perhaps more nearly, the last of his suppression of pessimism. In 1968 he confessed in print to the "deepest apprehensions" for the future of American civilization, and he spoke of "dangers" and a "threatening cloud":

> If the students think *they* are gloomy about the American scene, and fearful of America's future, I must tell them that they haven't seen anything yet. Not only do my apprehensions outclass theirs but my ideas of what would have to be done to put things to rights are far more radical than theirs.[33]

In this slightly ghoulish piece of one-upmanship lurks the key to Kennan's mounting distress: "what would have to be done." His views on democracy and decadence began to feed upon and reinforce each other. The antic inefficiencies of democratic government inspired scarce hopes in Kennan for the solution of pressing internal problems, just as the continued existence of those problems, in turn, confirmed him in a dark view of democractic government. Gradually, and not without horror, Kennan came to be convinced that the United States simply would not pull itself together in time. Unchecked, America's problems "spelled—it was plain—only failure and disaster."

> But what of the conceivable correctives? If these were to have any chance of being effective, would they not have to be so drastic, so unusual, so far-reaching in the demands they placed on governmental authority and society, that they would greatly exceed both the intellectual horizons of the American electorate and the existing constitutional and traditional powers of government in the United States? Would they not involve hardships and sacrifices most unlikely to be acceptable to any democratic electorate? Would they not come into the sharpest sort of conflict with commercial interests?

---

[33]Kennan, *Democracy and the Student Left*, pp. 228–29.

Would not their implementation require governmental powers which, as of the middle of the twentieth century, simply did not exist, and which no one as yet—least of all either of the two great political parties—had the faintest intention of creating?

This list of anguished questions (which, incidentally, went on for two pages more) led Kennan through his "Grand Inquisitor" dilemma and the search for a "middle ground" of meritocratic leadership within democracy.[34] When no "middle ground" presented itself, Kennan tried to return to foreign affairs.

But the exercise seemed increasingly, with the years, an empty one: for what use was there, I had to ask, in attempting to protect in its relations to others a society that was clearly failing in its relation to itself? It was under the pressure of this relentless question that I saw my public usefulness decline over the course of the years and tended more and more, so far as my own tastes and desires were concerned, to seek in the interpretation of history a usefulness I could not find in the interpretation of my own time.

And so where once Kennan had turned to history as a tool to influence the present, he now saw in it only the momentary boon of escape.[35]

The 1970s brought, therefore, just such stark cynicism as Kennan had deplored to Lasky in 1959. True, his 1976 letter to *Die Zeit* ended with something like a call to action, but it was more a bitter laugh than a rallying cry:

Poor old West: succumbing feebly, day by day, to its own decadence, sliding into debility on the slime of its own self-indulgent permissiveness . . . —and then trembling before the menace of the wicked Russians. . . . This persistent externalization of the sense of

---

[34]See Chapter 4.
[35]Kennan, *Memoirs* II, pp. 85–89.

danger—this persistent exaggeration of the threat from without and blindness to the threat from within: this is the symptom of some deep failure to come to terms with reality—and with one's self. If Western Europe could bring itself to think a little less about how defenseless it is in the face of the Russians, and a little more about what it is that it has to defend, I would feel more comfortable about its prospects for the future.[36]

"We talk of saving Western civilization when we talk of a military confrontation with Russia—but, saving it for what?" Kennan asked Urban at about the same time. "In order that 20 or 30 years hence we may run out of oil, and minerals, and food, and invite upon humanity a devastating conflict between the overpopulated and undernourished two-thirds of the world and ourselves?" Why bother, he nearly suggested: "I think this country is destined to succumb to failures which cannot be other than tragic and enormous in their scope."[37]

In the end, Kennan stepped back from this abyss, but only just barely. Should events continue on their present path, he said, "an absolutely certain ecological and demographic disaster . . . is going to overtake this planet. . . ." And moreover: "[T]here can be no real recovery from it. It is possible that some parts of humanity may survive it; but this would, at best, mean the beginning of a new Dark Age—all we have achieved in Western civilization over the last 2,000 years would be lost." There followed the barest *but*: "The decline of the West is not a fully accomplished fact, nor is our stumbling into this great physical catastrophe final. If we in the West could . . . think . . . of what is happening to our planet, and address ourselves, resolutely and rapidly, to preventing the catastrophe that looms before us, we would be doing a great deal better."[38]

---

[36]Letter to *Die Zeit*, translated and reprinted in *Decline of the West?* pp. 8–9.

[37]Kennan and Urban, "A Conversation," pp. 62, 3.

[38]Ibid., pp. 61–63.

III

Only with this background is it clear how little Kennan's changes of emphasis on the traditional issues of foreign affairs have to do with those traditional issues themselves. Little wonder that Kennan wants to cut and pare American commitments around the world; little wonder that he calls himself a "semi-isolationist"; little wonder that he is skeptical of moral pursuits in international life; little wonder that he finds democracy less than sacrosanct. Rome is burning. Kennan has less and less use for fiddles.

But is he right about all this? I think his prognosis bears a closer look.

To begin with, Kennan's argument on the decline of the West—despite all his lists of symptoms—is entirely unanalytic. It is like most everything Kennan has done: intuitive judgment, "non-communicable wisdom," "poetry." What Kennan wrote of his thesis in the X-Article applies just as well here: "This cannot be proved. And it cannot be disproved."[39] Or, in 1954, on the subject of decaying community relationships: "I am aware that there are experts on this subject who would deny that these conditions are really serious enough to warrant concentrated attention and recognition as a problem at the national level. But I can only voice a personal conviction that their significance for all of us is greater than we generally realize."[40] Kennan is a fine synthetic observer, and he follows in the tradition of de Tocqueville and the Marquis de Custine, whom he much admires.[41] But only history can judge judgments. Here in the present we have to come to our own, and it helps in comparing them to apply reason and premised argument.

To prove his case on the decline of the West, Kennan would have to do a great deal more than merely hand down

---

[39][Kennan], "The Sources of Soviet Conduct," p. 580.

[40]Kennan, *Realities of American Foreign Policy*, p. 113.

[41]See George F. Kennan, *The Marquis de Custine and his RUSSIA IN 1839* (Princeton: Princeton University Press, 1971).

a multiple indictment, like some sort of prosecutor. Every society, today and in history, has had its problems—as Kennan well knows. A stronger argument for the thesis of decadence, since Kennan seems now to believe it, might therefore be made through historical parallels, and Kennan does at least hint that America's ills are more like those of a dying than a flourishing culture. His frequent resort to quotations from Gibbon and his allusions to nineteenth-century Russian populists to describe present-day radical students[42] evoke, respectively, Rome and Tsarist Russia in decline. But these are only hints and evocations: never does Kennan openly compare and contrast these societies.

Hugh Seton-Watson, reacting to the Urban interview, disagreed with Kennan precisely on historical questions:

> [T]o say that, because all this [evil] exists, a society does not deserve to be defended, seems to me grotesque. This is not how nations, societies, and cultures have operated in the past. They worked; they defended themselves; they produced good and bad rulers, reformers and people resistant to reform; they grew and struggled and declined. And when they finally collapsed, it was because there was a combination of pressures from outside, and a loss of self-confidence by the educated class itself. . . . Take [America] as it is: it has warts and it has beauty. It has strengths and weaknesses. It does stupid things at times: many of its spokesmen are third-rate people, but politicians of all states include many mediocrities. . . . But why, for that reason, should one be ridden with guilt[?] . . . This seems to me an unhistorical way of looking at history.[43]

In other words, Kennan is doing just what he disliked in cynical novelists: exemplifying, and in some ways reinforc-

---

[42]Kennan, *Democracy and the Student Left*, pp. 150, 218.
[43]Hugh Seton-Watson, "George Kennan's Illusions: A Reply," *Encounter*, November 1976, reprinted in *Decline of the West?* p. 41.

ing, the phenomena of decline and despair even as he bemoans them.

This is, I cannot help thinking, Kennan at his worst: shaking his head sadly, wringing his hands, stirring a hopeless brew of ills and bad omens. A talent like Kennan's is wasted if it ceases—as, on the issue of American society, it pretty much has ceased—to give back in hope and suggestions for helpful change what it takes away in the finding of fault.

None of this is to deny the power of Kennan's analysis. The story here is the same as it was in discussions of strategy, morality, and democracy. I have nothing but admiration for Kennan's critical faculties, and he has few rivals in the definition of limits and costs. But the emphasis on the unanswerable diverts his attention from what *can* be answered. At some point it stops being constructive to point out the cloud lurking around every silver lining. "[H]ere again," to quote Kennan against Kennan, *"le mieux est l'ennemi du bien."*[44]

George Kennan gives the impression, in the end, of a very tired man. His has been the journey of an observer who always saw too much folly and tragedy for his own peace of mind. He began his career with a mission and a clear sense of America's limits and ills, but he is writing now with the gloom of a man who has failed in all attempts to transcend them. He is a gentleman and an aesthete in an often ungentlemanly and unaesthetic world, and the strain on his faith has been—perhaps—too much. I can think of no better reply to him than the one Walter Lippmann made to columnist Dorothy Thompson at a similar stage in her career:

> As for the future from now on—given all our mistakes and failures—I say: the devil with all catastrophic, apocalyptic visions of inexorable, inevitable doom. We may be able to avert it. Trying to avert it is the good

---

[44]See *Memoirs* II, p. 350.

fight—even if we lose it. . . . [W]e enlisted too long ago
to begin wringing our hands now.[45]

It is, of course, presumptuous to preach this way to a man of
Kennan's experience. But I sometimes think one determining difference between Kennan and me *is* experience—that
his career is more than half a century old while mine
(whatever it will be) has not even begun.

More than that, Kennan's values are showing their
years. A pastoral, agrarian society has much to recommend
it—and Kennan recommends it eloquently—but it is not the
society we have, and it was already history when Kennan
was born. To ponder its restoration is inevitably to tempt
despair and to conclude, as Kennan essentially has, that the
world is spoiled, like last week's groceries, and might just as
well be tossed out with the trash. Surely, that is more
crotchety than thoughtful. Kennan is not obliged to welcome
urban, industrial society; he can regret, if he likes, the
postwar proliferation of sovereignty around the world; he
can wish social mores had not changed and that democracy
were always consistent and full of good sense. But then he
must take account of realities, and look to make such
changes as can conceivably be made. To do anything else is
to be false to his own best tradition.

---

[45]Walter Lippmann to Dorothy Thompson, July 22, 1946, quoted in
Steel, *Walter Lippmann and the American Century*, p. 432.

Bibliography

Books by George F. Kennan

American Diplomacy: 1900–1950. New York, New American Library, 1951. [Includes reprints of both the X-Article and "America and the Russian Future" from *Foreign Affairs*.]

Realities of American Foreign Policy. [The Stafford Little Lecture Series.] Princeton, Princeton University Press, 1954. The Norton edition (New York, 1966) has a new foreword by the author.

Soviet–American Relations, 1917–1920 [Volume One]: *Russia Leaves the War*. Princeton, Princeton University Press, 1956.

Russia, the Atom and the West. [The BBC Reith Lectures.] New York, Harper & Brothers Publishers, 1957.

Soviet–American Relations, 1917–1920 [Volume Two]: *The Decision to Intervene*. Princeton, Princeton University Press, 1958.

Russia and the West under Lenin and Stalin. [The Chichele Lectures, Oxford.] Boston, Little, Brown and Co., 1960.

Soviet Foreign Policy, 1917–1941. Princeton, D. Van Nostrand Company, Inc., 1960.

On Dealing with the Communist World. [The Elihu Root Lectures.] New York, Harper & Row, 1964.

Memoirs, 1925–1950 [Volume One]. Boston, Little, Brown and Co., 1967.

Democracy and the Student Left. Boston, Little, Brown and Co., 1968.

From Prague after Munich: Diplomatic Papers 1938–1940. Princeton, Princeton University Press, 1968.

The Marquis de Custine and his RUSSIA IN 1839. Princeton, Princeton University Press, 1971.

Memoirs, 1950–1963 [Volume Two]. Boston, Little, Brown and Co., 1972.

The Cloud of Danger: Current Realities of American Foreign Policy. Boston, Little, Brown and Co., 1977.

The Decline of Bismarck's European Order [Volume One of *Franco–Russian Relations, 1875–1890*]. Princeton, Princeton University Press, 1979.

The Nuclear Delusion: Soviet–American Relations in the Atomic Age. New York, Pantheon, 1982.

Articles by George F. Kennan

[As "X"], "The Sources of Soviet Conduct." *Foreign Affairs*, July 1947. Pages 566–82.

"Current Problems in the Conduct of Foreign Policy." *The Department of State Bulletin*, May 15, 1950. Pages 741–51.

"Lectures on Foreign Policy." *Illinois Law Review*, January–February 1951. Beginning page 730.

"America and the Russian Future." *Foreign Affairs*, April 1951. Pages 351–70.

"Where Do You Stand on Communism?" *The New York Times Magazine*, May 27, 1951.

"American Troops in Russia: The True Record." *Atlantic Monthly*, January 1953. Pages 36–42.

"Training for Statesmanship." *Atlantic Monthly*, May 1953. Pages 40–43.

"The Nature of the Challenge." *The New Republic*, August 1953. Pages 9–12.

"Credo of a Civil Servant." *Princeton Alumni Weekly*, February 12, 1954. Pages 10–13.

"The Sisson Documents." *Journal of Modern History*, June 1956. Pages 130–54.

"When the Russians Rose Against the Czar." *The New York Times Magazine*, March 10, 1957. Beginning page 9.

"Disengagement Revisited." *Foreign Affairs*, January 1959. Pages 186–210.

"Our Aid to Russia: A Forgotten Chapter." *The New York Times Magazine*, July 19, 1959. Beginning page 8.

"History and Diplomacy as Viewed by a Diplomatist," in Stephen Kertesz and M. A. Fitzsimons, eds., *Diplomacy in a Changing World*. Notre Dame, University of Notre Dame Press, 1959.

"The Ethics of Anti-Communism." *University: A Princeton Quarterly*, Number 24, Spring 1965. Pages 3–5.

"Why Do I Hope?" *University: A Princeton Quarterly*, Number 29, Summer 1966. Pages 3–5.

"Peaceful Coexistence: A Western View." *Foreign Affairs*, October 1967. Pages 1–21.

"To Prevent a World Wasteland: A Proposal." *Foreign Affairs*, April 1970. Pages 401–13.

"What We've Lost in Vietnam." OUTLOOK section, *The Washington Post*, January 14, 1973.

"Reflections: Two Views of the Soviet Union." *The New Yorker*, November 2, 1981. Pages 54–62.

"On Nuclear War." *New York Review of Books*, January 21, 1982. Pages 8–12.

Published Interviews with George F. Kennan

Berger, Marilyn. "An Appeal for Thought." *The New York Times Magazine*, May 7, 1978. Beginning page 43.

Lasky, Melvin J. "A Conversation." [c.1959.] Reprinted in George F. Kennan, et al., *Encounters with Kennan: The Great Debate*. London, Frank Cass and Co., Ltd., 1979.

Kennan, George F. Appearance on *Meet the Press*. Washington, Kelley Press. January 3, 1982.

Severeid, Eric. "A Conversation with George Kennan." *Vital History Cassettes*. Encyclopedia Americana / CBS News Audio Resource Library. March 1975.

Urban, George, with George F. Kennan. "A Conversation." *Encounter*, September 1976. Reprinted in *Encounters with Kennan* and excerpted in Martin F. Herz, ed., *Decline of the West? George Kennan and His Critics*. Washington, Ethics and Public Policy Center, 1978.

"'X' Plus 25: Interview with George F. Kennan." *Foreign Policy*, Number 7, Summer 1972. Pages 5–21.

The George F. Kennan Papers
(Boxes 16, 17, 23)

"Measures Short of War (Diplomatic)." National War College, Washington. September 16, 1946.

Stenographic transcript, Lecture to Foreign Service and Department Personnel. Washington. September 17, 1946.

"Trust as a Factor in International Relations." Yale University. October 1, 1946.

"Structure of Internal Power in the U.S.S.R." National War College. October 10, 1946.

"Contemporary Soviet Diplomacy." National War College. October 22, 1946.

"Background of Current Russian Diplomatic Moves." National War College. December 10, 1946.

"Requirements of National Security." National Defense Committee, Chamber of Commerce, Washington. January 23, 1947.

"Russian-American Relations." University of Virginia, Charlottesville. February 20, 1947.

"Orientation and Comments on National Security Problem." National War College. March 14–28, 1947.

"Current Problems of Soviet–American Relations." Naval Academy, Annapolis. May 9, 1947.

"Planning of Foreign Policy." National War College. June 18, 1947.

"Soviet Diplomacy." National War College. October 6, 1947.

"What Is Policy?" National War College, December 18, 1947.

"Foreign Policy Aims and Military Requirements." Council on Foreign Relations. June 4, 1948.

"Where Are We Today?" National War College. December 21, 1948.

"Where Do We Stand?" National War College. December 21, 1949.

Other Primary Sources

Foreign Relations of the United States. Washington, Government Printing Office. Volumes cited are: 1946, VI; 1947, V; 1948, I, III; 1949, IX.

Kennan, George F. "Russia and the United States." [Pamphlet.] Stamford, Overbrook Press, 1950. [Reprints speech delivered May 27, 1950, in New York.]

———. Miscellaneous pamphlets, 1951–1953. Princeton, Princeton University Library.

———. Address before the Pennsylvania Bar Association. Manuscript. January 16, 1953. Princeton, Princeton University Library.

———."America After Vietnam." [Pamphlet.] Williamsburg, Colonial Williamsburg Press, 1968.

———. Remarks delivered on the occasion of receiving the Albert Einstein Peace Award. July–August 1981.

The New York Times. Various articles, 1947 to 1982.

The Washington Post. Various articles, 1947 to 1982.

Secondary Materials:
Books

Acheson, Dean. *Present at the Creation: My Years in the State Department.* New York, W. W. Norton & Co., 1969.

Barber, Joseph, ed. *The Containment of Soviet Expansion: A Report on the Views of Leading Citizens in Twenty-Four Cities.* New York, Council on Foreign Relations, 1951.

Beitz, Charles. *Political Theory and International Relations*. Princeton, Princeton University Press, 1979.

Bohlen, Charles E. *Witness to History, 1929-1969*. New York, W. W. Norton & Co., 1973.

Brodie, Bernard. *War & Politics*. New York, MacMillan Publishing Co., Inc., 1973.

Burnham, James. *Containment or Liberation? An Inquiry into the Aims of United States Foreign Policy*. New York, The John Day Company, 1952.

Carr, Edward Hallett. *What is History?* New York, Vintage Books, 1961.

Earle, E. M. *Makers of Modern Strategy: Military Thought from Machiavelli to Hitler*. Princeton, Princeton University Press, 1944.

Gaddis, John Lewis. *Strategies of Containment: A Critical Appraisal of Postwar American National Security Policy*. New York, Oxford University Press, 1982.

Herz, Martin F., ed. *Decline of the West? George Kennan and His Critics*. Washington, Ethics and Public Policy Center, 1978.

Kennan, George F., et al. *Encounters with Kennan: The Great Debate*. London, Frank Cass and Co., Ltd., 1979.

Kissinger, Henry. *White House Years*. Boston, Little, Brown and Co., 1979.

Lippmann, Walter. *The Cold War: A Study in U.S. Foreign Policy*. New York, Harper and Brothers Publishers, 1947.

Steel, Ronald. *Walter Lippmann and the American Century*. Boston, Little, Brown and Co., 1980.

Yergin, Daniel. *Shattered Peace*. Boston, Houghton Mifflin Co., 1977.

Secondary Materials:
Articles

Acheson, Dean. "The Illusion of Disengagement." *Foreign Affairs*, April 1958. Pages 371–82.

Lord Chalfont. "Why America Must Ignore This Man." *The Times*, May 2, 1978.

Gaddis, John Lewis. "Containment: A Reassessment." *Foreign Affairs*, July 1977. Pages 873–87.

Gati, Charles. "What Containment Meant." *Foreign Policy*, Summer 1972. Pages 22–40.

Halle, Louis. "George F. Kennan and the Common Mind." *Virginia Quarterly Review*, Winter 1969. Pages 46–57.

Kateb, George. "George F. Kennan: The Heart of a Diplomat." *Commentary*, January 1968. Pages 21–26.

Knight, Jonathan. "George Frost Kennan and the Study of American Foreign Policy: Some Critical Comments." *Western Political Quarterly*, March 1967. Pages 149–60.

Labedz, Leopold. "The Two Minds of George Kennan: How to Un-Learn from Experience." *Encounter*, April 1978.

———. "A Last Critique." *Encounter*, July 1978.

Luttwak, Edward N. "The Strange Case of George F. Kennan: From Containment to Isolationism." *Commentary*, November 1977.

Mark, Eduard. "What Kind of Containment?" in Thomas G. Paterson, ed., *Containment and the Cold War*. Reading, Massachusetts, Addison-Wesley Publishing Company, 1973.

————. "The Question of Containment: A Reply to John Lewis Gaddis." *Foreign Affairs*, January 1978. Pages 428–41.

Novak, Michael. "George X. Kennan versus George Y. Kennan." *The Washington Star*, December 29, 1977.

Rostow, Eugene V. "Searching for Kennan's Grand Design." *The Yale Law Journal*, June 1978. Pages 1527–48.

Seabury, Paul. "George Kennan vs. Mr. 'X': The Great Container Springs a Leak." *The New Republic*, December 16, 1981. Pages 17–20.

Sigal, Leon V. "Kennan's Cuts." *Foreign Policy*, Number 44, Fall 1981. Pages 70–81.

Steel, Ronald. "Russia, the West, and the Rest." *New York Review of Books*, July 14, 1977. Pages 19–22.

Taft, John. "Grey Eminences, X: A Diplomat for the Eighties." *The New Republic*, March 17, 1979. Pages 19–21.

Ullman, Richard H. "The 'Realities' of George F. Kennan." *Foreign Policy*, Number 28, Fall 1977. Pages 139–55.

Wright, C. Ben. "Mr. 'X' and Containment." *Slavic Review*, March 1976. Pages 1–31.

————. "A Reply to George F. Kennan." *Slavic Review*, Pages 318–20.

Index

About the Author

Barton Gellman is a graduate student in Politics at University College, Oxford, on a Rhodes Scholarship.

Mr. Gellman has spent summers covering local, national and international affairs for *The Washington Post, The Miami Herald, The New Republic,* and *National Journal.*

A summa cum laude graduate of Princeton University, Mr. Gellman majored in the Woodrow Wilson School of Public and International Affairs and was chairman (editor-in-chief) of *The Daily Princetonian.* His thesis on George Kennan shared the Myron T. Herrick Prize for the best Wilson School thesis of 1982.